MY KUNG FU MUSIC 2

BY THE AUTHOR OF MY KUNG FU STROKE

A MEMOIR OF SORTS

2nd Edition

GUY LE CLAIRE

GUY LE CLAIRE

Second Edition 2023 ISBN: 978-0-6454336-8-5

Cover Artwork: Guy Le Claire

Copyright © 2023 Guy Le Claire – mykungfu@yahoo.com

All Rights Reserved.

My House mate -Leigh Johnston (co - founder of Rose Tattoo), is urging me to call this book 'are we there yet', are we there yet. Are We There Yet - Jenny says "NO" and I don't.

are you there yet.

CONTENTS

FOREWORD 6
BIRTH: 7
GETTING STARTED: 1969 9
Learning the skills —-Academy of Guitar (Sydney) 1978-9
BERKLEE (Boston)1981 12
FREEFALLIN: 15
THE BANDS: 16
De bands cont' 19
14. JAZZ 20
GOING IT ALONE:1982 24
RAGING WATERS 1985: 32
EUROGLIDERS:1988 33
SYDNEY GUITARISTS 1980'S: 35
GEAR: 38
BOOZE/DRUGS: 39
IAN MOSS BAND 1988 40
RELEASE OF MY SOLO DEBUT CD 1991: 41
End of Oz touring... 44
more bands.. 45
PLAYDIEM 1987 - 1999 47
MATT FINISH 1990 & 2008 48
FREELANCING 1980 to 2014 50

BRUCE CALE AND GUY LE CLAIRE DUO1985-6	51
Biomechanics:	64
flashbacks	71
IN GOD WE TRUST:	72
MY KUNG FU Music One ~ Australia	73
FB 1976	76
MY KUNG FU Music ~ Hong Kong	78
GO BACK YOU ARE GOING THE WRONG WAY	83
Some of my Best Gigs:	87
ARE WE THERE YET?	91
THE END	94

FOREWORD

In a world that is so fucked up, it's easy to get on the negative. It was totes fucked for musicians! Especially during Covid. It is also difficult to decipher where music, artists & the business is heading. Creativity, expression & pathways appear to be stifled. However, I continue with this work in the HOPE of creating some good, positive vibes.

My physical Kung Fu (Tai Chi Qi Gong) practice continues daily, with morning work-outs in nature and occasional classes given to the community.

Having lived away from Australia for over 20 years (1976 to 1981 and then from 1996 to 2015), returning to my homeland permanently as a disabled person in 2015. Still armed with a mindset of pre-existing Aussie culture from the 1970's. I was a fossil, culturally fossilised, I am fossilised like a sort of dinosaur, I wasn't aware of the new protocols that had emerged over the past decades in Australia, I will say my first book was an enlightening experience.

With it unknowingly, I was going to express myself as a stroke survivor, hoping to share my recovery and optimism of following Chinese kung fu skill to my readers. Nevertheless I realise now I may have blind-sided some readers with my strong Aussie-ness of past times, in the 1st edition, it is what it is. My Kung Fu Stroke 2nd edition is now available all 'woken'. Here I will try my best to avoid my personal, romantic and private life with assumptions, and my family (who are innocent of all my endeavours).

This book is a replica of a time in music and professional music experience by an Aussie /Hong Konger from 1970 to 2023.

BIRTH:

Born 1960 in Sydney to actor parents. I am like an actor in a play, or a bigwig boxer going into battle, I used my acting and music skills to appropriate my employment. Along with reasonably good looks, I had developed a high level of guitar playing in my youth and I could see that by emulating certain idioms/genres and scenes in music (what I call stage roles) I would get busy re-employment. Chasing the dollar, I sold my soul somewhat... but who was GleC? (glec= guy le claire) a shallow or weak character from Crossroads? (the blues musician who sold his soul to the devil down at the Crossroads) No!

A talented musician and seeking dedicated guitarist who practised 12 hours a day, studied, took lessons, a burgeoning Master. Guy had been induced into the world of acting /drama by his two actor parents at birth and cunningly he could use their skill to be accepted into most situations/roles of Music. By playing roles.

In the beginning I didn't know, however if you wanted...

1. ROCK - I could Rock with me Cock!

2. Pop /funk - dance my little groove moves in tites and hairdos, no problem!

3. Jazz out- put on Salvoz jackets with a beret, grow a goatee Sving.

This last one (the jazz) would baffle me as I couldn't rip through changes. Standard songs. diu!

Australia, due to its English heritage & language capabilities, has since the World Wars been well connected to the United Kingdom and the United States of America, as it continues to do so. Aukus. These two super- powers influenced our culture and technology deeply. So it is a no brainer, that the germs of our music and art came from these two northern hemisphere places. Blues, Jazz, Rock, Country to Rap are now a part of Australian daily life.

'Music Oh Music, what have you done to me

i can't lose you or take you with me

o Music o Music

the Music to our ears'

Notes on book 1:The yellow stroke book;

My hope and aim was to instill some positivity and directives, with this book I like to think of it as a musicians handbook.. Kung Fu is a skill, developed over time. Most people have it and are Masters (potentially without knowing) - Musicians, Doctors, Health Professionals, Tech experts, Artists, Sportsmen and Women, Hospitality, Co-ordinators, Transportation workers, Police.

In other words all people working or dedicated to a passion!

You may not realise that within you is a Kung Fu….You Master (Sifu)! You need to work at it, not be hesitant/lazy!

I Kung Fu Master! :) when I studied Dick Russo's Jazz book he emphasised the importance of exercise, playing an athletic hobby, to get off music for a while. I agree.

GETTING STARTED: 1969

Air guitar on a tennis racket was my first foray into guitar.

Before my voice broke and measles, I sung well, I was singing all the time (but I couldn't understand the words sung by others after measles medication rendered me with a serious hearing defect) so at age 11, I began making up my own words singing over the top of Beatle songs. My favourite band! The influence and joy of the Beatles cannot be praised enough. The Fab 4 created such energy and excitement. Two guys on guitar strumming away, sensible economical bass work, propelled by the beat of the drums! and they could sing. I was hooked!

Each of the Fab4 were adored.

"the BEETS" were formed with best friends Marky Carr and Rolf Knudsen, we put on special shows for our parents and friends in living rooms playing our rackets and singing over the top of the record player playing the Beatles. Marky studied classical guitar in Vaucluse, Rolf was learning plectrum guitar in Mosman, both began sharing with me what they were learning, finally at age 12 Mum gave me a Kapok nylon acoustic to play on. Simon & Garfunkel plus flamenco records got played repeatedly as I tried to get it together on my guitar. While at Mona Vale primary age 9, a music day was scheduled with Alex Hood, he played guitar,

banjo and mandolin, sung and told Aussie folk stories, I was hooked by this journeyman's vibe and wanted to be like him. After the Beatles, Jimi Hendrix became my next huge influence. Jimi's "oneness" with the guitar, the sounds he coerced and his physicality, blew my little brain. Clearly there was a strong improvisatory element in Jimi's music, I was attracted to the self expressive creative potential of this, and you could say I have spent my whole life in an improvisation mode.

In addition to Jimi Hendrix.

Jeff Beck, Jimmy Page and Eric Clapton vied for top position. I was infatuated with the guitar, related to it big time. Psychologically speaking I don't know why but I loved it.

Later Santana exposed me to new notes within the pentatonic scale and rhythms, which I adored. Also my Chinese step-father Eddy adored Manitas De Plata (Spain), and flamenco entered my soul- I always felt like Flamenco was an emotional folk music like American Blues- I felt a correlation between the 2 and they featured guitar! (once down in Texas age 16 an African American homeless guy with a guitar, who looked like BB King began singing the blues to me on the street like a private show - I was mesmerised/hooked).

'Visions of the Emerald Beyond' by Mahavishnu Orchestra was played loud to me one arvo(1977) by my Mosman neighbours through their awesome sound system and it totally blew my brain. Here were two guys 'Devadip' Carlos Santana and 'Mahavishnu' John McLaughlin followers of guruji Sri Chimnoy creating incredible music, with blazing guitar ... Give me some of that!!! And Weather Report & Return to Forever! My parents played diverse music from Jazz to Ravi Shankar to Celtic Alain Stivell. World sounds surrounded me, leaving me often daydreaming.

Later in 1978 with school over, I took my guitar lessons seriously with Peter Andrews at the Academy of Guitar (Sydney), and learnt all the Modes -Major, Harmonic and jazz ascending Melodic Minors. When I obtained John Mclaughlin's book 'Mahavishnu Orchestra' I studied all the scales with Peter's help, unfortunately we weren't quite up on rhythm - so the piece in 20/8 or 9/8 was counted by me as 123456789/123456789. Incorrect. The way is to break it up into something like 123 123 123 or 1234 12 123. You can hear accents and the mind and mouth are not so overwhelmed by making smaller increments, it is manageable.

Because I never got this sort of guidance at the outset. Odd meter would always be a weak point in my playing, even-though I played with the greatest Australian drummers Andrew Gander & David Jones plus more. I mostly played by feel, unable to count 1234567891011 1234567891011. it is assumed I am somewhat of a rhythm expert, I am not, I worked by feel, only in later life did I become more aware.

Then one day (mid 70's) Mr. Biggers yelled down to John's basement where we were listening to Led Zeppelin loud and probably stoned, "Hey you guys come up here I want to play Guy this new guitarist!" On went George Benson's "Breezin" also on a superb sound system, At the end I didn't know what to think. But I did go to the State theatre with Rolf to see him (George Benson).

After which I was in total shock. I had to find out what all those notes in between were. Bop became a destination.

took me ages. My Aussie guitar heroes began with Kevin Borich his single "Tango Queen" tantalised me. with all the exposure to extra notes my study pathway was set in Jazz. And it was to be George Golla and Don (Burrows) Andrews that would set the example. Kevin Borich (KB) jammed with Carlos Santana at Rock Arena, he must be good! I studied with the great Ike Isaacs for a few years. Later in my career, I would jam big time with KB in Matt Finish. Local jazz guitar heroes Steve Brien, Steve McKenna & Steve Murphy influenced.

Strolling into Mosman Junction's record store after school (1978), the guy asked me have I heard this? Al DiMeola's "Elegant Gypsy" with a black Les Paul and a gorgeous lady on the album cover. After the opening track, I left with a copy under my arms. The modes had reached a new plateau! Power driven by a Les Paul through a Marshall!

By 1974, a needed routine in life developed, all my high school years was Mosman High. Along with compadres Chris Frazier(professional musician), Tony Buck(the Necks), Tom Ellard(Severed Heads), Doug Ironside(Matt Finish/artist),Greg Ohlback(pro drummer), Rolf Knudsen (artist, creative musician), and a cast of many - Ralph Hague, Macy, Dugald Brown, Simon Baderle, Dikran Balian, Brett Curotta, Steve Mason we all dived into Led Zep, Deep Purple, Band of Gypsies, the Doors & Cream. Mosman high was a groovy place!

Trying to figure out the grooves and head spaces of these remarkable British and American Musical Masters, along with the intensity and improv(improvisation) involved and relevant social reflections... blew my brain apart. Later as I discover Sydney's guitar talent, I will be inspired to reach new heights as well as have a good base & training ground and a moniker by which to gauge my progress.

Living with Dad on Avenue Rd., Mosman, I often skateboarded down Ballantyne St., noticing a boy about my age, John Maurici sitting on his fence looking at me. I had heard drums edging out from his garage, at times his brother Tony banging away with his mate guitarist Stephen Conlon, John and I got talking and agreed upon having a play, he on the drums, me plugged into Stephen Conlon's amp. We did and loved it, we chatted about our favourite band THE BEATLES. and got to work.

I think at John's 21st birthday party in his garage, we played for the party, no idea what we played! Probably Tony sat in with brother Chris on bass, we ended up drunk, jamming.

Besides John becoming my best mate, he was a bit unco, and his drumming didn't quite keep up with the Mosman cats from my school, Greg and Neil Ohlback, Tony Buck, Simon Baderle, Steve Mason and Alex being hip young cats following in the John Bonham/Cobham tradition.

In addition out the back of my block of flats (which faced John's backyard) I pummelled a tree -kung fu style- nightly after seeing "5 fingers of death"(1973) and training with Felizardo. However music was beginning to take hold of me, over my other Kung Fus - surfing, skiing- I was going to make a "go" of it (music), but I knew, due to my inquisitive nature, I needed to learn the music language. I wasn't particularly great at covers and working out the guitar parts (additionally I was quite deaf having about 80% hearing after measles), so I began composing my own little ditties "Afternoon Sun', 'Los Tres'. Los Tres was a little trio put together with brother Chris Frazier 1974.

Unfortunately, the little home-made band disbanded at a gig in Balgowlah, with me going off my head in true GleC fashion.

Learning the skills —-Academy of Guitar (Sydney) 1978-9 BERKLEE (Boston)1981

starting out on guitar: 1972

I did find Rolf and Marky to be learning quickly as they took lessons. Rolf seemed to be aware of the hot guitarists Clapton, Beck and Page, emulating Johnny Winter, and chords and licks... how did he know all this stuff? this is what a good teacher does.

Cosmos Factory, Grand Funk Railway, Hendrix, Cream, Led Zeppelin, Santana, The Doors, Deep Purple. Being tutored by Peter Andrews introduced me to the necessity of good technique, scalar work & sightreading skills.

USA/BERKLEE: 1981

Boston, being exposed to Pat Martino, John Scofield, Pat Metheny and witnessing Mike Stern was beyond incredible.

not only their soloing, but their composition had strong affect/impact on me too. The chord sequences and melodic material scalped me. My little Amin pentatonic capabilities were being unbelievably expanded.

The Berklee College of Music ran a number of adds in 'Guitar Player' magazine, one add featured one of my favourite guitarists - Al Di Meola— with him stating 'I went to Berklee so should you'. When I received my application it said 'what/who was your recommendation to apply'? I put down Al Di Meola and got in. Upon arrival you are auditioned and placed in appropriate classes.

I only managed one semester, cause I was on limited funds, but oh boy! what a semester! Mike Stern/ Ken Taft, guitar excellent workshops. Mick Goodrick, Randy Roos, met Pat Metheny and sat with him in one of the clubs. Fellow senior student Kevin Daley (Minnesota) was in my opinion the best guitarist that semester, after a few jam sessions with Kevin, in which I flopped bigtime, he then became my teacher, plugging most holes and queries, I practised six hours a day EVERY DAY. My roommate alto-ist Black Ben from Denver, modeled himself on and looked like Charlie 'Bird' Parker. Be Bop became a necessity. Once while hanging outside our room, I asked the guy with smokes' have you got a spare fag?'— Ben looked at me with his big brown eyes and pulled me aside saying 'don't be sayin' shit like that, otherwise you'll find some guy humpin' you right up yo ass". Other stories included the Kiwi student who at dinner in the canteen had all these blokes gathered around his table, I went over to see what all the commotion was about, he was advising the best way to fuck sheep! The Americans were in awe.

I got to see Mike Stern playing often, I loved his swagger with his Fender, bit of chorus and distortion playing bop style rootsy blues inflected lines with a consistent swing in 8ths or 16ths. I had no idea what he was doing, I wanted to be able to do it. Later I achieved something akin. As I was leaving to go to Paris then back to Hong Kong, I bought the 'Berklee Correspondence Course'. Back in Hong Kong I completed the 25 lesson "Berklee Correspondence Course". Benny (the trumpet player at Ned Kelly's HK) was always so proud to state he had completed the correspondence course. We nursed our Certificates proudly.

After which I hoped to get into the Sydney Conservatorium Jazz course. Don and George were my auditors, when Don looked at my big band score he exclaimed that "hey this big band arrangement lacks shit 1st of all the parts on the score are in concert, they should be in transposition." I then lost my mojo, shaking and terribly nervous I tried to respond to their audition requests fucking it up. The summer Con jazz clinic put on in 1981 was awesome with Hal Galper, Freddie Hubbard and ECM drummer Jon Christensen… plus meeting and connecting with some of Sydney's finest.

It was good.

The Jazz world had reigned me in, I was hooked like a kung fu. I wanted to exist in this jazz world!

Today I really believe that scoring music, working on jazz improvisation develops life problem solving skills. Music in schools!!! I'm ALL FOR IT!!! It has helped me with brain injury to deal with many aspects presented in life.

Also at my stage now, I hear phrases played in key (inside) then repeated up in another interval(outside). Training the ear to work in these boundaries is quite liberating. The key is to resolve outside to inside, thus reflecting life i.e. orgasms.

custom laid, letter jane it's my aeroplane

songbird lame in de pain it's my aeroplane

music is my aeroplane that mother fuckers always filled with pain.

r.h.c.p/glec

FREEFALLIN:

King rat puckered up before his team of vermin "C'mon we'll infiltrate this home where old incapacitated rockers live (Guy & Leigh) and seek a feast"

they all scurried offending many delights, until finally old mother hen Rat keeled over after ingesting blue pellet food exclaiming she'd at least seen the blood moon!

I remember being born and a few hours before thinking are we there yet? Time & gravity necessitated that I was to arrive in this story you may find some issues dealing with your own stuff like my first book, well I'm now at the end of this one - I been there, so the next phase is ahead and I wonder ' are we there yet"…

These were the highflying tour days - jets, hire cars, tour managers and stage roadies. A far cry from the early days of driving, driving, driving - are we there yet? - like the first pro band I joined.

Freefallin!Cont'.

I am part of the Eurogliders, we are flying to Sydney on a Fokker East West jet from Queensland. The night before Sydney was pummelled by a damaging shock storm, we enter the assembly of storm clouds stretching from left to right, down to up, as far as the eye can see, the ensuing barrage of jerks, drops and bumps made Luna Park feel like a toy as we entered this hostile airspace.

It is in this free falling moment that I was exposed to my inner optimism and HOPE. Positive experience in the face of death, I believe this inner energy has guided me through some rough times in my life, enabling me to smile at the other side And be thankful..

THE BANDS:

FAIRSTAR SOUTH PACIFIC 1979:

the FAIRSTAR cruise ship. With Mike Hague -drums, Steve Hunter/replaced by Stan Mobbs -bass and Manuel Das Neves- vocals strange accordion keyboard.

French /Algerian Manuel had been hiring me for his French restaurant gigs, I needed the money. He was in with some agents and they booked him to lead a band of myself -guitar, Stan Mobbs/Steve Hunter - bass, Mike Hague - drums and Manuel on a sussed electric accordion and singing, in the Fairstar's dance room, alternating with the main band in the Starlight lounge a reading band (the Starlight Orchestra) that backed up imported acts, the house band featured Eric, Bob Donaldson, Mark Costa and Tony Barnard. The dance band/our band- stilted by its repertoire- left a lot to be desired, sometimes it was downright embarrassing, however good times were had sailing around the South Pacific on a grand old lady. Sleeping in after constant late nights, then crawling up to the deck, with only the sea and the flat line of a horizon to view (which drives you bonky after a time), by the afternoon I would descend into the ships bowels to the cinema in search of trees, land and mountains and where "For Your Eyes Only" set in the magnificence of Europe, 007 played on rotation. Here I saw Greek vistas, Swiss mountains and something I could identify with. I must have watched it 100 times! Long live 007!

One of the overlooked aspects of living on the east coast of Australia is our pacific neighbours, Fiji, NZ, New Caledonia, and Vanuatu. The 'Nesia's' Polynesia micro etc. Remembering pics and school topics on such area, brings back images of Fijian police officers with white gloves, French Cafes and slurping mud pools. Not to mention our northern neighbours - Indonesia and all of SE Asia (Austronesia). We live in a rich cultural exchange area!

The ole Fairstar would depart from Circular Quay right smack bang in the centre of Sydney Harbour and City, we sailed out late arvoz, reversing under the bridge and Luna Park, then forward past Fort Denison and my ole stomp Mosman Bay, Taronga zoo and out past the North and South Heads and out into the wild ocean of unknown, and the night and the music.

FOR SALE BAND.1984:

Gerry Day (front man/vocal), Will Scarlet (front man/vocal), Bob Wynyard (leader guitar/vox/1770) Steve Merta (drum/vocal/Anketell forest), Dario Bortolin (bass/ Baby Animals), Glec, Bongo - American sound guy who upon waking up, drew on his trusted "Bong" stayed with us all the way.

Steve O was one of those cats that always got a good sound out of his drums - I was spoilt early, he constantly fiddled with the drum tuning and mic placement and PA - what a dude! plus he sang really well- he could a joined Barnesy!.

Dario had just come out of Van Halen type band of which his mate guitarist was John forget his name John was Sydney's most highest exponent of Eddie V..I was challenged with all my Berklee training, however there began my deep appreciation of Eddie Van Halen RIP and God bless him! I was nicknamed "BP" – the quiet achiever.

We drove from Sydney to Uluru via Tenant Creek NT, Mt Isa, Longreach and Charleville (where I fell asleep) and back via Tenant Creek/Warrigo Mines, Rockhampton and a snow laden Armidale. Are we there yet!?on high rotation!`

Expecting to open the Uluru Resort, on a certain date. The Resort kept delaying the date, luckily the boss of Telford's Alice hotel(where we played) liked the band and extended our stay continuously. We met some extraordinary characters, quite mind boggling, one good looking girl reckoned she had bonked NSW premier in Gold coast and was running away from cctv footage... stories went on and on, as it became clear that the Uluru resort would not open anytime soon we decided after 3 months in Alice that we better head home, via Tenant Creek again playing in nearby Warrigo mines, for the miners and families, a strange place with just a massive round hole in the ground the miners had to be elevated down into. after the gig Dario and I are in the kitchen of the after gig party and a miner (still with his hard hat on) comes over, offering a joint? yeh why not it's been a long tour & the end of a rather unusual time (the NT is like another country, I am blown out) after a few tokes me and Daz are super high, then the mousy little miner begins singing the Disney 'M-I-C-KEY M-O-USE Mickey Mouse, Mickey Mouse' song. Basically he summed up our 3 months stuck there and Daz and me freak-out!:)

Once we thought -thanks to the fat agent prick - we were playing in Adelaide, after driving all night- are we there yet?

We couldn't find our venue, so we had to wait around until old fatso got up to find out where we were to play 'oh Telford's Whyalla.' fuck Why alla!!!? probably one of the top shit towns in Oz. 8 hours later we made it, to see in the backstage area written on the wall Susie had fucked Daryll, so & so had fucked so & so. Weird.

In summary, the NT experience exposed me to a whole Australian world I had never encountered. A mind expansionist thing. The drive back to Sydney was full of Are we there Yets!!!!?

.I existed in an artistic endeavour in my mind and dreams – in a desire to make 'my' music. But with a mindset stuck in Chinese pragmatism paradigm. Money, Money la!(boring!),I didn't pursue my art. I believed in a pathway of Miles, Mahavishnu, Weather Report these musics were showcasing original music, musicians and reflecting society at that point, especially Miles' music became so futuristic, one could easily imagine they were in a rocketship headed for space!!! Listen to 1960's Miles' it's far out! Heres an album I did on my tascam 4 track... I am beginning to find my voice…from the vault of 70s

https://guyleclaire.bandcamp.com/album/rock-king

In fact, I was getting ready to go to NYC and join Miles' band.

I wanted to participate in a creative original artistic thingo. That came much later after hanging with like-minded individuals who were doing it! & retrieving universal God inspiration/guidance which continues to this moment.

With the passing of David Gulpilil a few days ago, I was acutely reminded of my very white North Shore upbringing, no awareness of the black indigenous Australian community, or anything really. It was like we all lived in a bubble – fucked/unreal. Play chillis Walkabout...But David connected me to his people and culture through his efforts (and Archie Roach) right throughout my youth and adult life. So David I remember you forever and here is my little shrine to you. I love you. And thank you. As the sun goes down we remember you and all the brilliant Australians!

De bands cont'

12. THE TRIBE: 1986

Led by Kiwi Jan Preston keys vocal leader, with Maori Mina Moto on Drums and Aussie Gary Evans on bass, the band had a record deal with CBS/Australia records and was off-side managed by Chris Murphy of INXS fame. Later Phil Witchett keys joined.

Going off to a Jade rehearsal with Dave Marsalis in a new rehearsal centre near Rushcutter's Bay, running late. I squeeze into the lift with petite Jan and warrior Mina, they ask do I play guitar? 'Yes' they just lost their guitarist and have a new album coming out on CBS. An audition is booked at the Darlinghurst squats. I get the gig.

Australia's music scene was at this time coming into it's own with the Oils, Inxs, Chisel, Icehouse. I would say the English punk thing had morphed with the 70s pop glam thing and keyboards, along with a strong American pop element. This formula seemed to have settled in Australia. Here in our country the influence of Great Britain and the United States of America steered Oz through- big time!

Tribe an original band, had these elements with a dose of tribalism.

For My tenure with the Tribe 1985-87 I wouldn't see any moolah, luckily there was the dole and private teaching. I was playing a fender squire strat, through a Marshall combo with extensive use of a TS-9., this band kind of transformed me into a Rocker role - blonde, mo hawks /makeup, tights, and attitude. I enjoyed this role.

This would be my path and again later with the Ega Ninjas.

The Tribe have been booked to open and close (yes play a set after the main act!) for John Lydon's **PIL at the Tivoli**. Johnny was rotten to the core, an arrogant evil incarnate, which was amplified and after our first opening set, Gary pulls out a splif and lights up, I drag on it, then Gary says "c'mon let's go watch from the lighting area above the stage". we settle there then the marijuana kicks in ...Rotten appears and says "right fucking orstrallia" makes a huge sound - coughing up phlegm, then spits it out at the audience. They go wild spitting back.

The band begins its smack addled post punk funk pop malcolm mclaren esque NY crap.

What I saw above culminated in my belief that Rotten was possessed by the Devil. Then we had to play a closing set. CBS fuckwits idea no doubt! - absurd - ducking between globules of spit on the stage floor. I couldn't wait for it to end.

Clearly the Tribe wasn't gonna get real big, and with stifled creative energy we just fizzled out. I don't even know what I did after.

Post-punk band The Tribe formed in Australia in the early 1980s, with New Zealander Jan Preston as their charismatic frontwoman. Spearheaded by Preston and drummer Mina Motu, the band were joined by Guy Le Claire on guitar, Gary Evans on bass and Phil Wichett on keyboards. Preston, a classically trained pianist, had previously performed with Kiwi band Coup D'Etat and theatre troupe Red Mole. In the early 80s, The Tribe released two EPs — War Cry and Even In Russia — and singles 'Angel of The Junkheap' and 'Dreams'. Preston went on to a prolific solo career in Australia as a jazz and blues artist, as well as composing for the screen.

Guy Le Claire established himself as a guitarist in Hong Kong.- rock history oz.

* * *

14. JAZZ

As I am not a professor or writing a thesis doc here I will as a stroker take the liberty here as to how I think Jazz entered the Australian, and perhaps Hong Kong psyche. Very early jazz encouraged dancing which like a fad spread the world over. The music was lively, happy and jazzed up with co-related dance moves.

Dixieland/Traditional Jazz and dance moves -big band music gave way to ballroom dancing all this was the popular culture of the time (1920s through to 1950s), later Latin American music and dance would sweep the world, proving music knows no barriers or borders. Hollywood was a powerful American propaganda machine. Here in Australia we spoke the same language (eventhough they spoke with an accent), we fought world wars together and developed a brotherhood and respect. When movies such as 'High Society' hit the screens down-under, we were smitten with Louis Armstrong and Cole Porter's music with Frank Sinatra, Grace Kelly and Fred Astaire along with the leading ladies. These characters etched their way into our hearts through many more movies like An American in Paris, On the Town, Top Hat. In fact, when I was 11 at Mona Vale Primary School I began sobbing in the playground when I heard Satchmo (Louis Armstrong) had died.

Jazz musicians are skilled professional musoz.

WHY JAZZ MUSICIANS WERE HIRED SO MUCH FOR STUDIO WORK:

Record producers went out of their way to hire the finest most-experienced Jazz musicians with their great playing techniques (perfect for recording) right from the popular 100 or so jazz clubs around in the LA/So. LA/Hollywood, South-Bay Coast areas in 1957-58 to play/invent lines on the rock-pop-soul record dates from then on, including most of the 1960s. No-one knew how to write "rock arrangements" but they knew jazz musicians could invent for any style, that's what we did every night, with every note of soloing, and comping behind solos, no problem. Plus Rock was beginning to take over the former prolific jazz clubs and we saw the hand-writing on the wall, most of us who had a family to support....

Record dates paid much better. Most of the recording musicians who did your fav hits were Jazz musicians....those who weren't fouled up on drugs/booze simply moved over to do record dates, eager and glad to get the work, and we found we liked this

"new music" even tho' we had to dumb down to invent the right lines for it all - personal likes and dislikes didn't matter, it was a clean good business to record every day and night....it was fun and enjoyable for many a year before the surf-ennui started to set in later in the 1960s....There's only so long you play/record that surf music day and night without getting bored....

Anyway, it was a long run and we all enjoyed creating/making those hit records - you should have heard the music *before* we invented lines to it and played it....what you all hear is the final product, *after* we did our job....and yes, we're all proud of our work, we're all from the work-ethic years of doing a good job for the client, accounts we used to call them....it's a business, not "our personal play-ground" - in LA you had 100s of studio musicians working every day in recording records, doing movie scores, TV-film show recordings back then...our Musicians Union, all 2 vast floors of offices were going day and night to keep up with the contracts.

I was the first one (actually the 2nd one, Barney Kessel was 1st) to quit doing record dates in 1969, like someone said "you're at the top of the heap, why quit?"....he didn't understand that music is important to me, it all started to sound like cardboard music. I needed to go out to play with Joe Pass and then Hampton Hawes to play some real jazz again, this time on bass.....but in 1970, I did go back to do the movie scores and TV-shows films I had been doing since 1963 but no more rock, pop, or motown dates no....had enough of all that, only so long you can go with no sleep and was tired of playing rock and roll, I needed to get back to my roots: Jazz, or at least as close to it with Joe Pass and Hampton Hawes.

There were fine arrangers like Perry Botkin, and later Jack Nitzchie (protege of HB Barnum probably the only one who could write arrangements back then) and also Jimmy Haskell etc. who quickly caught on from what the studio musicians would invent (a lot of the time they learned that way - this is not to take away from their great arranging chops, but rock-pop-soul etc. were different and growing idioms back then - the jazz musicians were the first to psyche it all out and invent the right lines for hit records, the ear-training we all had was invaluable (standards and jazz).........One time, I even saw Gene Page write down my invented bass lines only to "sightread" them 2-3 weeks later!)...but by the mid 1960s we all had to start "sightreading" more and more....no problem for the jazz and/or former big-band musician.

But it was about this time that Glen Campbell and Leon Russell were starting to have problems "reading charts" because more and more it was tougher lines all the time. Funny how we all started to work for THEM as they moved on up to be stars....because they couldn't sight-read notes...! They became stars instead ....they highly deserved their success, they were EXCELLENT musicians with so much natural talent.

Jack Nitzsche:

* * *

An aspect I found stimulating was hanging with Jazz musoz. They explored all manner of music. World musics, Jazz, Classical very aware & open minded musoz. Researching, discussing, sharing. A positive engagement. The passion! & professionalism.

Jazz musoz continue to blow me out with their command of instrument, knowledge, awareness, wisdom & their music!

The Philadelphia Story

by Philip Barry

Produced by   Sol C. Siegel

Starring

Bing Crosby

Grace Kelly

Frank Sinatra

Cinematography   Paul Vogel

Edited by   Ralph E. Winters

Music by   Cole Porter

Production

companies

Sol C. Siegel Productions

Bing Crosby Productio.Distributed by   Metro-Goldwyn-Mayer

Release date

July 17, 1956

George Benson 'I started out on the blues New Orleans blues each chord had a feeling'.

I fink I figured it,,, black musoz played the blues from their being, the ole french euro music infiltrated the local sounds w harmony & compostional/improv approaches... jazz is a blend of black & euro music!!! Jungle music!

' how to get the most out of the melody' gb

One of the few things in life that give me immense pleasure is improvising (harmonically) through a set of chords to a jazz standard. It's almost like playing chess with the tune (although I don't actually play chess) It requires knowledge and experience, strategy, poetry, dynamics, drama, tension and release. And then there's the tactile nature of actually playing the guitar. The 'massaging' (or forcefully extracting) notes from the strings! It's a beautiful thing! And the reward is 'music'! Anyway, here's a quick run through "Body & Soul"! May you enjoy! Jeremy Sawkins.

***

GOING IT ALONE:1982

The summer Con jazz clinic put on in 1981 I met and connected with some of Sydney's finest upcoming young jazzers.

It was good.

The Jazz world had reigned me in, I was hooked like a kung fu. I wanted to exist in this jazz world!

JAZZ Cont':

getting with swinging eighths was a challenge trying to get the phrasing right. Don Burrows has that.

I've just spent the last week listening to the "Don Burrows Collection" over & over and what a romantic lyrical magical player along with his comrade George Golla. I had a gripe with these two previously as I was knocked out of getting into the Con, however today I wish I could tell the Don how much I dig and respect him for what he is. That won't be possible as he suffered a stroke (don't I know about that!) and currently resides in heaven. Thanks Don! my paths forward by this stage are as an independent determined artist. I have been to Berklee & moved forward regardless and I wrote 2 books and released over 20 CDs! max.

The tasking and planning involved with jazz guitar is beyond comprehension, the decisions and pathways.

Will I play it/ the head in this octave/key or that one? I noticed Pat Martino plays heads in middle register/middle strings allowing him to embellish on high or low strings around, creating interest and tension. Pat Metheny has a tendency to play heads (head is the melody of the tune) up an octave reinforced by his wonderful keys player Lyle Mays. This gives Metheny a vocal, floating like ambience. Decisions, decisions!!!? And after that goddamn blistering BlaineO, Dayle sax solo now what do I do aaaaaaaaaaaaaaaaaaaaaaaaaaaaaaaaaaaaaaaaaaaa!!???

Jim Hall had a slow, non-resolved approach, leaving us hanging, bit like Thelonius Monk.

i bet Monk's coffin was heavy.

"You have to be able to play, but I think the desire is half the battle, and then you have to put it in action. I used to walk around thinking I really want to be a jazz guitar player. And there I was – I spent half my life not playing jazz, just to make a buck. I used to wonder all the time "Why can't I?" -- well it's because I wasn't doing it. It takes some sacrifice. If that's what 17.you want to do, play jazz guitar or sculpt people's faces out of marble, or whatever you want to do, at some point in your life you have to say this is what I want to do and you have to go do it. Nobody's going to come over and say "Poof! Here's $10,000. Go make records." I used to hope for that, but that was being totally unrealistic. That's what made it happen – when I stopped playing all the rotten jobs and only when I played what I wanted to play. That's when it happened." Jimmy Brunos

This is why I stayed in Hong Kong so long, and loved the place because, I was making a buck playing Jazz! god damn it!, My creative musical achievements were all based in Jazz, and I made a good living, allowing me to practically do anything I wanted. HK was awesome! Tall poppy syndroming is not a HK thing generally. Not to mention HK is one of the planets' most incredible city.

Another positive, was Jazz had no gender or sexuality issue. In addition I dug Chinese Culture and chicks.

* * *

Know vamps intros & outros.

Chord progs.

Tonal movement.

Cycles hey joe 5ths

4ths root movement

Timbre

Syncopation some of these topics are looked at later.

"should emphasis be placed on the notes while improvising, or the rhythm?" Scott Tinky.

* * *

Master DALE BARLOW: renowned jazz musician.

I have had the good fortune to tour with Dale at least half a dozen times in Hong Kong, Macau and China. Once after a great gig in Macau we hopped in a taxi (me, Dale, Peter Lee, Anthony Fernandes, Sylvain Gagnon) Me and Dale broke out in our Gander Glec sheep noises, going over the top, the cabbie freaked out and the sound was transferred to Sylvain forever. The next day Dale and I got a cab from Macau to Guangzhou, 150ks, only in China, actually it was quite a scenic ride. As an experienced travelling Aussie with a good time feel, and earnest. Dale took me on for all his Asian sojourns, if two of us could play then the pickup ensemble, no matter how bad would sound passable, there were some corkers though, bloody hard to get through. The best time was had when we settled in Taipei, Taiwan (me, Dale, Nicholas McBride- drums, Alan Dargin- didge), here I noticed Dale incrementally teaching and sharing to me his world of Jazz, I began to feel like George Golla and George Van Eps all rolled into one. We did record in some strange place in Taipei, and the record "NOMADS" was released later.

Dale is a musical Master. it was a privilege.

* * *

'Why is jazz not part of the pop scene anymore?

Herbie Hancock - Because it's not the music that matters anymore.

People don't care about the music itself anymore, but about who makes the music.

The public is more interested in celebrities and how a certain artist is famous than music.

16.It changed the way the audience relates to music.

They no longer have a transcendental connection to music and its quality.

Just want the glamour.

Jazz doesn't want to be part of it.

Do you know why?

It's not about humility, or arrogance, a posture " we don't want to be famous, we're underground ".

None of that.

Jazz is about the human soul, not about the appearance.

Jazz has values, teaches to live the moment, work together, and especially to respect the next. When musicians gather to play together, you have to respect and understand what the other does.

Jazz in particular is an international language that represents freedom, because of its roots in slavery.

Jazz makes people feel good about themselves.'

- Herbie Hancock

Acid Jazz (??)- the pop/rock commercial freelance musicians I worked with blew my mind, in so much as they could recreate sound, transcribe songs well, and had really incredible memory retaining intellect. However they really had no idea about "Real" jazz - hence the culmination and invention of Acid Jazz I think.

A lot of these musoz didn't profess to.

Pseudo jazz

a robotiqueness/ machine like/ society image

we will be overcome by robots.

bass grooves / 2 chord monotony- no Mc Coy here.

Codal/Modal – systems revealed to make it through unusual musical compositions can be advantageous. Codes.

Bands continued...

GLEC QUARTET 1981:

https://guyleclaire.bandcamp.com/album/le-claire-quintet-rsvp-2

Andrew Gander - drums, Steve Hunter - bass, Kevin Hunt- keys, Jason Morphett - sax. I knew I needed a recording of my band to chase up gigs and promote - things were getting tight financially, but I managed to pull us all together for a recording at the "Atlantics" studio in Earlwood. The cassette album I released enabled me to score some gigs, namely Jenny's Wine Bar in the city and the Ultimo hotel thanks to my teacher Ike Isaacs.

Steve and I wrote all the material. It was a very fine ensemble of extremely talented young musicians (each member went on to become Australia's top player) and I feel the album sounds fresh 40 years later today. It is on my Band Camp. I was playing an Ibanez A200 through a music man amp, with a tube screamer and the old boss chorus CE-1. The track 'H805515' was my guitars serial number. later I purchased an Ibanez AH10 Holdsworth.

The Sydney Jazz scene was awash with talent and gigs popped up everywhere, The Sydney Conservatorium of Music (the con) led by Don Burrows was graduating many young fine jazzers.

Venues such as the Basement, The Paradise Jazz Cellar, Soup Plus, Jenny's Wine Bar existed with jazz most nights, groups such as Keys Music Assoc. and S.I.M.A.(Sydney improvised Music Assoc.) put on shows in churches, trade union clubs, and other cool venues. The inner city flourished with weekly gigs in pubs, bars & cafes.

Clearly having the ability to write out charts was a win win situation, it swiped time off rehearsing and if the participating musician couldn't remember, they had their chart, for instant performance. I'm pleased I had the ability to do this as I definitely wouldn't have such a large catalogue of my music if it wasn't for charts & readers.

THEM OR US: 1980's

https://guyleclaire.bandcamp.com/album/them-or-us-1

Geoff Lungren - bass, mini- keyboard, samples, vocal, Midi

Bill Heckenberg - drums, vocal, percussion

GleC - guitar, vocal, FX

This was the epitome of my existence in the 80s with Geoff and Bill, I was finally able to participate in music, that was in me - the funk- Prince, the rock - Vai, Satch, the prog - Belew/ soundscapes -.Varese, the jazz, we got together with no preplanned or arranged thingo, no charts. Unlike Geoff's fave Zappa, I liked Frank, especially his puppet video and guitar playing, but I found his voice annoying so I never really got into him. Them or Us just jammed for hours at Bills place above the Harold Park in Glebe, I recorded everything on my walkman. Later splicing it up to create tunes/musical pieces and our repertoire. Both Geoff and I took turns in lead vocals, Geoff being the better half.

Geoff and I met and gelled in the Nic Clarke days. We lived in the Mosman/ Cremorne area.

Them or Us were the first band ever to play "The Harbourside Brasserie". Scott Howlett from Juke on that occasion gave us a tremendously brilliant review, in fact the INXS boys would come down to listen, after a hard day in Rhino, recording KICK. As well as other notables.

Geoff was one of the first guys to use midi bass, his arsenal consisted of a sampler he triggered with his feet and multiple fx. Geoff is a genius, too far ahead and intelligent for the times we lived in, often misunderstood. I was playing my beloved Fender Mustang (I sprayed silver with locking whammy) through a vast array of fx namely delays and distortion (Rat) through a Marshall 100w combo- real loud!

"Beard" on the Them Or Us my band camp was recorded by Peter Cobbin at studios 301, Peter would sneak us in on dusk to dawn sessions, giving us studio experience and the like.

We sometimes went under Pseudonyms, one being "Merrylands". I began chasing the dollar, and Them Or Us became extinct. Also I think as Geoff and I were pursuing stable relationships- getting married, kids etc. this band as much as it had rock star status, couldn't quite live upto that status. As potential rock stars tended to be drugged up/booze addled free fucking mutha fuckaz, and we weren't that. Clearly we weren't sex gods, writing romantic ditties. We were 3 serious young men. And two of us were seeking stable relationships and needed a more secure way of providing what lay ahead.

EGA NINJAS:1986-87

Jim Pealing - singer/songwriter

Bill Jacobi - bass

Tom Kennedy - keys

Stuart Henderson - drums

gleC - guitar

Jim Pealing reminiscing via messenger…

"Being an old hipster from the 70's, it was hard to get my head beneath the hairstyle of the 80's. But it had to be done to be accepted into that era of fashion. The Ega Ninjas were formed to comply with the gel of the day. Total Fire Band were a wonderful experience of music. But the band wanted to dive into the pool of modernity. They hired me. Probably because I had the right haircut.

Total Fire Band were on the go when I moved to Sydney from Adelaide around 1985. I came over to join a band called "Magna Carta". We lived in Paddington. The guitarist was Gwin Ashton. The other two guys were from a band called Venom. It went down the dunny. 🚽

Anyway, the drummer mentioned to me that Total Fire Band were looking for a singer. I applied. These guys had a huge following. As soon as I joined, they all fucked off. I thought if we stuck at it, we may have achieved some success. It appears that total fire band became Ega Ninjas.

Guy your song "Secrets" was great. Have you a copy? It's a tune I haven't got. Your guitar playing in The Ninjas was superb. Hats off to ya, man.

James

James Pealing

🙄

Sun 17:23

You sent

Darn we dedicated ourselves to les ninjas. Dear Henry was one of ur masterpiece z

I remember didja brush ya teeth

James Pealing

Yeah. Dear Henry. I've got a lot of tunes in that same vein. Incontinent Lament, I can't get away from my arse etc.....

Bill and Tom were in TFB. They were great. The lead singer was quite a character. Mick Hawke was his name. Great guy. Charisma a-plenty. I think it was a real shame that the guys ended the band just to become more trendy. They were big. People loved them.

I joined the Ninjas around 86 🥺

So we was 86 to 87. In that studio near de RPS with Stuart. Who was fat agent guy pooping in and promising de bs

Sun 18:36

James Pealing

Anthony Conlan? Yeah. The fat fuck suggested we play some covers. We did and it fucked up our potential credibility. Oh well. Ya live and loin. Camperdown was the suburb we rehearsed. I'll never forget that time when you Kung Fu'd those dogs out the front of the warehouse. Remember? They were attacking a smaller dog. You marched straight in like a praying(preying?) mantis and sorted them out. Legendary. I've spread that story all around the globe. People listen in awe.

***

We covered a few U2 tunes (indeed we had a bit of a U2 vibe), this allowed me to explore their music and Edge's guitar approach in depth. It was an enlightening opportunity. I was playing a black Ibanez Roadstar with delays and overdrive can't remember the amps. We rehearsed mon-fri like a job, a bit like the dog Sam & Ralph clocking in, we would in our Camperdown rehearsal space. clock out at 5. Somehow we pulled together a covers repertoire (U2, Gabriel, Talking Heads etc.), And an original repertoire. Not sure what we were thinking… except earning a bit of dough by fat fucks cover band rooms. We worked hard and juggling five young men's beings wasn't always easy, but we did it for a good while. Now I can't even remember what happened to us, although we remained friends.

RAGING WATERS 1985:

Justin Dileo - bass and charts. Justin got this band going along with Afro-American singer now based in Sydney - Armondo Hurley.

We began with Stuart Henderson drums later taken over by Chris Sweeney (the Sween), Mark Kennedy, then Kerry Buchanan, along with bass subbing by Mark Costa and Ron Francois, Geoff Lungren. Keys players that drifted in and out were Peter Rundle, Paul Najar, Raj Kamahl - culminating in a residency at the fancy Riva Nightclub City after having maintained gigs in Manly, North Sydney and The All Nations Club the X.

By this stage Australia has been through the disco period and the soul/funk hits of the 70s and 80s have become somewhat 'standard' with most people knowing Stevie Wonder, Earth, Wind & Fire, Chaka Khan, Prince etc. These artists became our source of repertoire including RnB standards like My Girl, RESPECT, Get on up, Hold on I'm coming:)

Armondo, was a man on a mission to perform his heritage music to Sydney audiences. We had our followers and at times pumped the whole room, what a gas!

I began living and taking a new stage role in a fantasy of a Black World of beautiful black ladies, their music and their black musician counterparts, later in Hong Kong I would hang continuously with my Black Brothers we made some bad-ass music up there.

It was a super learning curve for me as I donned my funk guitar role and due to Mauritian blood, exceeded.

In addition, meeting and playing with Sydney's finest commercial musicians. The pay wasn't bad either, with my teaching and a working partner, we began eyeing to buy property.

With this band I got with the great funk guitarists Al McKay (EW&F) and Nile Rodgers (Chic), loosening up my right rhythm hand and letting it skank/ funk out. Learning by listening and studying Hot Licks instructional videos. We played Afro- American hits/funk and Soul with some sophisticated Al Jarreau, James Brown and Tower of Power. Including the ever great Michael Jackson, Janet Jackson, E,W&F. It was my training ground and I really enjoyed it!

EUROGLIDERS:1988

Led by song writers/vocalists Grace Knight and Bernie Lynch, this Euros incarnation number 2 featured Sydney's Finest. Euros #1 fell apart prior to heading into the studio to record "Groove" album - Bernie assembled a stellar cast of musicians - Stuart Fraser/gtr, Craig Calhoun/bass and Chris Sweeney/drums to carry the recording project through, it was released in March, 1988.

I went into the band with my white Jeff Beck strat, running in stereo through a little peavey bandit (clean transistor sound) and a 100w Marshall combo (for a bit of grunt)- Rex and I got sponsored by Casio synth guitars with EMGs (I never used it much live- too heavy for me to bop around with my dance moves, but used heaps in a songwriting spree done on my Tascam 4 track). https://guyleclaire.bandcamp.com/album/leclairevoyeurnt-tunes

Finally I got an Ibanez RG550. That would become my main axe.

The Eurogliders toured nationally for three years under the guidance of Kevin Jacobsen- Glebe. It was an incredible live band, with some of Oz's best/talented musicians.

Phil Witchett (RIP) from Doug Williams and Power - the Paddo Green days/ practically coming when Doug did "That Girl" with Phil squirting out those those massive key chords in the chorus! Lindsay Jehan a session ace - allrounder/awesome electric bass - had studied some Lydian Chromatic thingo, Tech ace, vocals and keyboard bass -important for 80s pop bands. Steve Sowerby - drummer straight out of Richard Clapton along with another thing. Incredible attack on drum set and time.

Rex Goh top Singapore born Australian Electric guitarist. Did the Con, learnt the shit, loves Robben Ford. Had been a part of Air Supply and QED. Additionally recording the Tribes album "War Cry", then tutoring this young author at a Tribe rehearsal in the Darlinghurst squats on chords used and sounds. Kind man…

Along with Rob Henry sound man extraordinaire, and tour manager. Rob setup awesome monitoring. Placing emphasis on amps etc invalid. focussing more on guitar fx/simulators through direct inbox to the system, this was my era.

Not to forget the bubbling talents of leaders Bernie Lynch - guitar/vocals and Grace Knight - lead vocal.

These were the high-flying tour days - jets, hire cars, tour managers and stage roadies. A far cry from the early days of driving, driving, driving - are we there yet? - like the first pro band i joined.

* * *

SYDNEY GUITARISTS 1980'S:

Azo Bell- Azo was co-founder of the Keys Music Association propagating contemporary jazz he played an angular unusual guitar style I was attracted to, we played together in Rated X (Paul Andrews/Pete Dehlsen/Sandy Evans/ Jez Sawkins/M Palumbo),

Ben Butler - a young Canberran who played well and exuded style and grace,

the 3 Steves - Steve Brien - friggin awesome guitarist on the Sydney scene in the 80's then left for USA.

Steve Murphy- used to see him at the basement after my Monday evening guitar session at the Academy of Guitar, as I was at the Quay would pop into the Basement to check him out. Tele rock bop expert. Disappeared. Steve McKenna (RIP) a graduate of LA's Musician's Institute, McKenna and Murphy would often play duo at the Soup Plus. I was there every time. Peter O'Mara- expert based in Germany. Jim Purnell- Jim appeared due to Diane Spence, Dieter Kleeman- used to see Dieter playing in the Jupiter band on Sundays at French's Wine bar, was always in total awe of him, Jim Kelly - Crossfire master Red335 in style,

Jeremy Sawkins, TIm Rollinson - Jeremy and Tim shared "the hang" house Green St., Paddo with my mate Tony Buck I was round there all the time, we jammed a bit and I always admired Tim's - Jim Hall-esque approach and Jez's modern playing and compositions we often would walk to the X to check out the Paradise Jazz club,

Peter Northcote - modern Aussie guitar at its best, Rex Goh - top notch electric guitarist, our careers entwined right throughout the 80's (he a member Air Supply, QED, Euros) we played together in the Eurogliders. Ken Francis - Session king, Tom Ferris - reader and shows, Dev Gopalasamy - Oz Indian guruji, John Stuart- mountain man on a mission, Stuart Fraser (RIP) - Noiseworks and the works, Steve Edmonds- broad blues based slinger, Mal Eastick- blues in stereo, Steve Williams - Adelaide funkster (Wa Wa Nee). James Muller- Adelaide Master - James flipped everyone out when he moved to Sydney!, Dave Smith- Swinging in the modern world, Finbar O'Hanlon- Fin is an inspirational individual always curious and pushing the boundaries of Rock we worked together at AIM, Ike Isaacs - Ike from London became my teacher and mentor in 1986 I dug his passion and devotion to jazz guitar we worked together along with Dave Smith (and most of these above guitarists) at AIM, George Golla, Don Andrews - George and Don I feel are the true Aussie jazzers of Guitar they were literate doing gigs and sessions left right and centre eventually teaming up to create the Academy of guitar where I went in 1979, John Robinson- from Blackfeather to Cremorne, Kirk L'Orange Canadian born sifu, Bob Spencer- Angelic rocker we used to jam in the mountains, Kevin Borich - KB blew me out when i was pre-teen with the La DeDas and "Tango Queen" KB toured with Matt Finish 2007 We jammed on the last tune 'Fade Away' Big time really rocking out!, Chris Brown - Ayers Rock,

Carl Orr- another Adelaide Master, Nathan Cavaleri -young gun, Phil Stone- early shredder, Johnny Nicol- on the scene, Peter Inglis- education and art, Brad Johns- Neutral Bay Primary to now, Matt Hanley- hot tradie of the coast, Doug Clarke - Sunburst Music, Bruce Mathiske don't know this Bruce, Steve and Jak Housden-wonderful players, Dave Colton- London ahoy!, Tony Barnard- goodbye UK, Ian & Nigel Date- well hello Ireland, Louie Shelton- the wrecking crew LA, Mossy, Moginie, Peter Boothman,

Tony Elwood forget fripp let's flip the guitar, Guy Strazzullo - European passion finding the soul, Peter Zografaikis-didn't know Zog but he could play!, Jason Campbell-met JC at the summer jazz con clinic '81 we clicked and it was pretty obvious that he lived for "BOP", John Baker - softly spoken kiwi dude I met outside the one truth gig at state theatre, Chuck Morgan – jazzer.

Jamie Wilson- winner guitar battle Selina's I was a judge along with Jeff skunk Baxter, Dave Dwyer- don't know Dave, Maddy Young - sweet jazzer gone too soon, Parish Muhuberac – rich heritage, Les Rankin - matt finish lege, Lex Wilson from Manzil Room this was a guy you knew could play!, Joseph Calderazzo- dont know Jo, Paul Berton- Creative rocker, Dave Leslie - Baby Animals, Dieter Kleeman, Dave Hole – come for a ride on me slide, Mark Lizotte - aka Johnny Diesel - exceptional, Jeff Lang - don't know jeff, Eric Rasmussen- funk, Mark Punch - Renee Geyer expert, Dai Pritchard, Scott Leishman, Dave Brewer - don't know Dave, Arnie from Jump Back Jack, Les Gock – from Hush to jingles, Mark Plumb, Clive Lendich.

So many...

And the phenomena of Tommy & James & Angus Young -

Angus, darn! what a guitarist and innovator, the hookiest chords and riffs ever.

Tommy Emmanuel, no music college for this incredible talent, how'd he do it!? Tommy plays everything i don't want to.-

but, darn the boy can play! but where did he learn all those harmonies? and technique? no going to Vienna, Madrid or NYC to study, what a chap! What a performer!

we all love Tommy!

James Muller, incredible modern electric guitarist, probably plays everything i want to:).

EVH. Vai and Satch - As I progressed playing wise, in order to survive in Oz the necessity of retrieving various current sounds in conjunction with playing ability led me to Steve Vai and Joe Satriani, hells bells Berklee my school was involved! As these guys are alumni. Vai is an Alien, Joe is a lovely down to earth guy I met and gave my debut cd demo to, he mailed me back a very encouraging letter.

when you sit down to think about it.

The Electric guitar advanced in an extraordinarily fast time period. In seven decades it morphed from strummee big band role or some Chicago Blues records to a leading unrestricted voice with Charlie Christian/Wes Montgomery to the Shadows/ Elvis and to the Beatles. UK pop and US recordings began featuring the guitar if not the guitarist right from the 1950s, 60's and 70's.The 1980's pop scene saw it's decline to a part player as keyboards and technology held sway. However the future greats like Steve Vai and Joe Satriani and Eric Johnson inspired by the masters like Hendrix, Clapton, Beck and Page, continuing with recent masters Edie Van Halen, Yngwie Malmsteen, Michael Hedges, Zappa, Benson along with a wider appreciation of Jazz and Blues and all music in general I would say, the new cats blossomed in their bedrooms and garages. Reading up and listening to current rock, blues, jazz and classical techniques, experimenting- eventually coming up with a spectacular approach to the instrument and composition.

For example on guitar it is now standard ability to play pull offs/hammer ons flowing into legato phrases, awareness of rhythmic placement -forward motion accented by the great Eddie. Scalar knowledge- Modes and their related moods and nuances, tapping. It's really incredible considering it mostly began with the blues and pentatonic.

GEAR:

even though I grew up in Mosman/ North Shore, Dad and I weren't wealthy, there began a struggle to buy/access good music gear, this is maintained to today. I have a cuppola Artist guitars I like, a little Joyo amp, I began with an Ibanez Artist A 200 and a music man combo as a pro this sufficed until I got busy in major rock bands & sessions…

Growing up in an affluent Sydney suburb my fellow cats seemed to have good gear Fenders/ Gibsons etc. But I felt I needed to learn the guitar well and exude my playing through my hands and fingers. So, gear was out no money la unfortunately pretty much until I stopped touring 1990.

Living in Montreal, Canada at age 16 (1976) I got a job working with a car park cleaner, rising at 4am to get out to work, I was able to buy a White Aria strat that looked just like Jimi at Rainbow Bridge!

Later got Ibanez Artist A 200 and a music man combo as a pro this sufficed until I got busy in major rock bands & sessions…

Also Dad wasn't very tech tradie- ish, no man sheds out the back in Mosman! so I inherited that, meaning I wasn't techie, a guitar luthier type, I just wanted to know how to play it real well… hence I used luthiers and repairers. A lot of kids had the knack to make things - slingshots, animal traps, lego etc, I did not possess those qualities. Plus I was deaf as…

The biggest joke is that guitarists buy/spend large amounts of money for all their gear, plus a vehicle to cart it around, only to turn up for a $50 gig! Potentially not a wise business investment?

BOOZE/DRUGS:

It was not uncommon that these two existed in all music roles /genres—alcohol and marijuana being the most used.

Stage fright - loss of confidence may have something to do with it, in addition to brainwashing youth culture.

My take on it is … Everything in Moderation. try Chinese Kung Fu, find your own Kung Fu!!! Kung fu is just a skill acquired over time not fighting like the song. diu!

Kung fu means skill developed over time.

Self - Employment:

Self-employment is the state of working for oneself rather than an employer. Generally, tax authorities will view a person as self-employed if the person chooses to be recognised as such, or is generating income such that the person is required to file a tax return under legislation in the relevant jurisdiction. Sole trader.

if you are out going it alone, it would be wise I feel to get an ABN (Australian Business Number) & TAX FILE Number. The Musicians that had it during the pandemic/lockdown managed to secure some government payouts.

My career was becoming more of a tradesman, than a pure musician, I personally felt my music skill set was being pursued for things other than my own artistic endeavour. I was selling my wares like a true whore and having the Hong Kong Chinese money pressure, was limiting and narrow. (I am married to a HKer at this time).

Suddenly I needed the latest gear & gizmos to recreate the latest sounds and keep up with de joneses, it became a silly cycle. I could only act so much, then you're confronted with delivering the goods.

As life and family held sway over my ability to spend, I never had the opportunity to buy gear at leisure so I resorted to the 80's cart around a rack / for Gigs and sessions, until twenty years later, I had spare dough in Hong Kong, where I got everything pretty much I wanted.

see below…

Notable story in my mind is Tommy Emmanuel calls me to sub on Jim Kelly for a gig at the UNSW campus. I load up me Citroen CX2400 with the sovtek and peavey and rack, thinking I got a good rig! We play a tune before Tommy comes on with Tele and straight into a red nosed Twin. His sound soars cutting through the whole band whilst mine was a mish mash of shit. He told me later he got 2 JBLs put in it and you couldn't lift it up. Within a month I bought the exact same amp from Fender, Oz.

That was one heavy muthafucka.

IAN MOSS BAND 1988

Rebekah Johnson the bassist in 'Hip Hop, a funk cover band featuring herself, Peter Northcote, Paul Joseph, Rav Kamal. Rebekah was touring with Mossy. I was subbing for the ever busy Peter Northcote in Hip Hop, me and Reb developed a strong friendship and musical rapport. Mossy was known to be hiring and firing as he clearly couldn't find a suitable players to make his music. Reb highly recommended me for the next tour. 1987 an Audition was organised, and I got the gig as rhythm guitarist along with Ian Belton (bass) No Rebekah! diu!, Steve Fearnley (drums), Danny D'Costa (keys), Mark Williams and MaryAzoppardi (back-up vocals)

. I completed a whole tour on a good wage and was booked to do a second tour this time with Chisel drummer Steve Prestwich. We toured nationally and when Ian's album "Matchbook" debuted at number one in the Oz charts, we went live on MTV, playing most of the album 1988.

Hearing Ian Mossy play every night and sharing the stage with him was a true delight. I kept my head low, just sticking to my guitar parts/role. Not trying to get in the way or my playing ability out, trying my best to support/contribute to his music.

In Jindabyne Ian was carving up a solo out on the front walkway when in a lull he waved and motioned me to join him out of the blue on said walkway to trade licks. I did and as Ian was encouraging me, I let rip! Back in my spot on the stage the kids below began yelling -"who's that guy!!??"

I never got booked again no 3rd tour, I was out and the Oz touring scene was crashing. Al Yaaaaa!!!!!!!!!!!!!!!!!!!!!!!

RELEASE OF MY SOLO DEBUT CD 1991:

Naturally I thought this is an album worthy of adding to the musical spheres, taking 10 k out of dad's account since he was felled by a delapidating stroke, I pursued my dream. I must say if not for the help of Mr. John Prior and Mr. Lindasy Jehan - co producers and engineers, plus the talented musicians involved, this whole project would not have scene the light of day.

Simply put it was basically my instrumental story, reflecting guitar techniques evolved upto the day – blues, jazz, shred, Vai, Satch, Holdsworth, saturated in rock, funk, prog, jazz and storytelling. Them or Us personnel made appearances on a few tracks, as well as some GleC quartet dudes, along with Sydney's top music talent. Thank you!

John and Lindz played on most of it. The debut release garnered me media praise and landed me a publishing deal/advance from pmt music/Polydor. I composed all the music and liaised all the recording sessions.

John and Lindz knew I was part deaf, and mentioned to me when something was humming or not right, I needed these 2 brothers in the studio. Upon the release I gained more confidence to tackle the music world as a solo artist, rather than hiding in bands with outcomes dictated by leaders whom may not know. I was in charge of myself! oh what a feeling GLEC!.

Probably the first review was by Michael Smith from On the Street, a positive review along the lines of this talented guy probably won't get a nice fat advance from any record company (true) but oh gosh this CD is good. Reminds me of yesterdays post on FB, a successful footballer earns more per year than it cost to support an Orchestra. darn Aussie!!!!

Bridge Hotel - Allan Holdsworth support act, With the Cd out I got booked to open for Allan at the Bridge Hotel, every brilliant Sydney musician was there, and I got the jitters so bad my left hand was shaking uncontrollably. I didn't think I could do the gig. Nervous as all fuck! We jumped up me shaking I just looked at Mark the drummer (Radiators) with his long hair, double kick drum and twiddling sticks and Bill pumpin' away on bass and got into the zone, and did it!

Guitar World features and Sonics, On The Street did stories.

I have not mentioned THE BLUES yet, as a whitey suburban Aussie I was pretty ignorant of rock music's beginnings, however I became engrossed with blues guitar back to front. Beginning with Larry Carlton, then lending my red nosed Twin to fave Robben Ford. I was hooked on these guys, later I would back up at least two dozen blues acts at the Hong Kong jazz club. the rhythm would

en-trance me, as simple as it is, the infectious shuffle, preliminary to swing I reckon and the circular form going round and round created a trance state, when one was right into it. True Trance in the Zone stuff.

Today I listen to Muddy Waters and Freddie King & T Bone mostly.

My kung fu music.

There was no greater feeling then ripping out a phrase or jazz lines with alternate picking and feeling that right hand plucking on the strings with your left-hand coordinated fretting these incredible lines as well as chugging along to a great feel.

Ultimately I consider myself jazz musician.

What are you going to play if somebody asked you to just play a drumstick solo, guitar solo, violin solo? I think you need to come up with a plan. And then because there was such brilliant guitarist Tommy Emmanuel etc playing covers and doing beautiful renditions of them my approach was to create my own music, to be able to play the guitar the way I wanted to with my own music. Also there was the incredible feeling of physically being with the instrument.

FELT that I had developed a solo show of my music incorporating all elements of feelings because I believe that musicians and artists reflectors of society and so by the time I had released my third album I'm in my solo three album, was ready to take on the world and then I played Fringe club Hong Kong so if you see that on YouTube and so then I was ready to take on the world that God would smash me down with a stroke and I wouldn't be able to play.

When around 1960 Davis bought the building at 312 West 77th Street in Manhattan, a five-story former Russian Orthodox church, he put a music room and a gym in the basement. There he'd begin his days jumping rope, doing bag work, and using a rowing machine. "You have to have rhythm and good time to do both," he said, comparing boxing to music. "Doing exercise makes you think clear and your blood circulate. It makes you think stronger, feel stronger, and you can play whatever instrument you play with greater strength, whether it's right or wrong." Boxing, he said, was "like practicing a musical instrument; you have to keep practicing, over and over again."

He saw in boxing the flow state—that feeling of energized, focused immersion that can transform or slow time, leaving more room to engage both intellect and instinct, or bringing a sense of ease and play to split-second reactions. The flow state—the hyperfocus that race-car drivers also search for—provides common ground in horseback riding, fast cars, boxing, and musical improvisation.

Michael Bloomfield: "When I was 17, I thought I was good enough to gig in black places and hold my own. You had to hold your own. If you shucked, then you had no business being there. You'd not only be a white kid, you'd be a fool. You'd be a punk and a fool....Several guys took me to be almost like I was their son—Big Joe Williams, Sunnyland Slim, and Otis Spann. They took me to be like their kid, man; they just showed me from the heart. They took me aside and said, 'You can play, man. Don't be shy. Get up there and play.' What I learned from them was invaluable. A way of life, a way of thinking, a whole kind of thing—invaluable things to learn. I used to hear Elmore James, Sonny Boy, Little Walter, Howlin' Wolf, Muddy Waters, Freddie King, Albert King—way before they were known anywhere but the ghetto....I was interested in it from a musicological standpoint. I was trying to discover where the old blues singers lived. I met cats like Washboard Sam and Jazz Gillum and Tommy McClennan and Kokomo Arnold. I used to have a band with Big Joe Williams....By then it was a scholarly thing. Like Paul Oliver and Sam Charters, I wanted to know the story of the blues, and the best way for me to learn was to actually meet the guys."

From: Michael Bloomfield - If You Love These Blues: An Oral History by Jan Mark Wolkin and Bill Keenum

The term race record, initially used by the music industry for African-American music, was replaced by the term rhythm and blues. This rapidly evolving market was mirrored by Billboard magazine's Rhythm and Blues chart. This marketing strategy reinforced trends in urban blues music such as the use of electric instruments and amplification and the generalization of the blues beat, the blues shuffle, which became ubiquitous in rhythm and blues (R&B). This commercial stream had important consequences for blues music, which, together with jazz and gospel music, became a component of R&B.

As I got older I researched Blues and loved the two Kings - Albert and Freddie, Wolf, Hooker and Waters.

End of Oz touring...

BLUE MOUNTAINS 1987-1996

A move to Katoomba in the Blue Mountains to settle down and facilitate housing my expanding family and a better lifestyle.

Australian Institute of Music 1987 – 1996

Being interviewed by Dr. Peter Calvo (a man whom I had respect an elegant Gentleman) and Daniel Calvo his son in an office smack bang in Sydney CBD was a little unsettling after years on the road. My tenure with the touring big bands had ended, I was there…for the time being, no more are we there yet. I had released my first Solo CD "Guy Le Claire" gathering positive press (Guitar World magazine USA featured me in the new talent page). The interview with the Calvos went well, I then trundled off back to Katoomba on the train. It was confirmed that I would be the Head of the Guitar department - currently running at about 20 full-time students. A massive advertising campaign was to follow over the next few months before semester began. In addition, I was to put together a teaching team and curriculum. Immediately I booked Carl Orr (a fellow Berklee dude) and Jeremy Sawkins (a Syd jazz con graduate) liaising with these two fine gents on curricula, enabling me to put together a full two year - full time Diploma of Music program/curriculum.

By the time the semester started we had over one hundred full-time students. The vision had gone through the roof!

I had to recruit more teachers, besides my own teaching to make money (I was not remunerated as head of guitar as such just given my hourly teaching rate and I suppose the power to book myself as many hours as possible), I found myself running the guitar department working with many lovely guitarists and musicians. It was hard work and much responsibility. We the teachers, followed the curricula and produced some very fine players. By memory Haydyn Walker, Dan Silk, Iwayan Balawan, Jason Winn, Chris Brooks, Russell Nelson, to name a few.

My musical outlets at the time were Zilch and Playdiem. this all lasted until 1996 at which point I moved overseas to live in Hong Kong.

* * *

The Australian government Education Dpt. began getting heavy weighing down on teachers without qualifications.

Peter Calvo called a meeting, it was agreed I would Study for a Diploma of music, thus my pathway in the classical world began… studying conducting with Nikolai Sokolov and familiarising myself with orchestral instruments.

My jazz studies had given me only a certificate of music and knowledge of Big Bands - horns and rhythm section, excluding delicate instruments like celeste, harp, the string and woodwind families.

TIMBRE is the quality of the voice or instrument. Something we could all take into consideration. Sound or tone. Tone colour or sound quality.

I enjoyed this 2 year study period, obtaining my diploma in 1994. Later in HK I got a jazz guitar performance diploma from the mobile London College of Music. (they and others send their examiners out to test long distance students-moi).

* * *

more bands...

ZILCH 1988 - 1990

Formed in Katoomba, Blue Mountains with mates.

Gary Evans (RIP) - bass Gary held a creative vision of good music and visual arts we bonded real well in the Tribe, both having Asian wives and musically complimentary,

Boof/ Ray Husband - vocals. Boof first came into my life on the Fairstar as part of "Family Affair" a brilliant Maori family ensemble showcasing Afro- American popular music.

Frank Corby - drums, I came across Frank through Mum and her Main St. Market, a fellow Berklee dude we got playing! I played my ibanez RG 550 through the rack and a couple of amps, we mostly played RnB classics and Red Hot Chilli tunes along with our own songs.

We fucking kicked arse in the mountains! awesome band! John Hogan hardcore fan!

by this time in Australia, the shred guitar syndrome had peaked and gone, bands like Jane's Addiction and Red Hot Chilli Peppers held sway. Also the classic RnB repertoire had become standard. Zilch played on these genres along with healthy doses of Hendrix. Gary Rowley was our dedicated sound guy.

SOUND GUYS: Sound Engineers are vitally important for bands as is the sound system (PA), along with their mixing capabilities, sound guys and their rigs can actually make or break a band.

foh- front of house - the main rig, speaker system faces the audience, a tower of speakers/ foldback- the speakers on stage facing the singer and band so they can hear. Big bands, have both a foh sound engineer and a foldback mixer.

by this time popular music was becoming very parts oriented, improvising spontaneity had left the building

the Stones with Keith created the guitar parts of sus4 chords as recognisable parts, inxs rallied on this with similar approaches funkified.

the instruments had lost their spontaneity with quantised drums and shit....A session often required the musician to come up with a part the Producer liked, then polish that part rhythmically/note wise and commit to tape.

Katoomba: After I left Oz Gary Evans organised jam sessions at Tres Elies with Frank Corby, Len Marks, Mick Young, Hamish, Make. by all accounts these were well received and good fun.on ya Gary!

Today there are some good players up here

Bruce Cale, Brendon Coleman - guitar, Jo Truman - vox, Liam Grey - gtr, Bill Crossland- bass, Isaac Beggs-drum, John Stuart - everything, brothers Adrian & Rupert, Oliver Morley-Sattler - drum, Tubby Wadsworth-drum, George Gerontakos-dbass, Hamish Reinharhdt-gtr, Len Marks-gtr, Jason Thornton-sax, Shiheeda, Boris Hunt-tpt, Loyd Swanton-dbass, Brett Hirst- dbass, Col Day- gtr, Red Bee featuring 'champs' Daniel Silk- gtr/vox. I don't play anymore so i don't know all. just what i've seen…

Sorry if I missed ya.

PLAYDIEM 1987 - 1999

Playdiem was started by me and my good friend at the time Steve Hunter, Steve coerced me to call David Jones (drums) and John Foreman(keys) to see if they would be interested to have a play with a view to making a band.

When four of Australia's most impressive jazz musicians get to play together the audience can certainly expect the unexpected and that's exactly what **PLAYDIEM** deliver! The music on this album is refreshingly innovative (they're all originals) and further evidence that Australian jazz musicians can stand tall with the rest of the world and even deliver music that stands taller! Guy Le Claire and Steve Hunter are both acknowledged as leading stylists of the guitar and bass respectively whilst David Jones has often been described as 'the drummers drummer' and John Foreman, although a recent graduate from the Sydney Conservatorium on Music, is already recognised as one of the country's leading pianist. It wouldn't be an understatement (or record company hype) to say that this recording is chock full of real music and great music at that.

1. Hong Kong	G. Leclaire	3.15
2. Third Avenue	G. Leclaire / S. Hunter	3.05
3. Girl On The Moon	S. Hunter	6.41
4. Dedication	G. Leclaire	5.11
5. Ride The Camel	S. Hunter	5.27
6. Isabel	S. Hunter	4.47
7. Dragon Fly	G. Leclaire	8.14
8. Space Cadet	S. Hunter	6.35
9. Zatorio	G. Leclaire	2.50

Produced by **Guy Le Claire** & **Steve Hunter**
Engineered by **Alex Wong** & **Mark Don** at Paradise Studios and Studio X, Sydney in January & April 1993
Mastered by **Steve Smart** at Studio 301

Special thanks & love to our families & Friends.
Thanks also to Alex Wong, Bill Fields - Paradise Studios, A.I.M., Mark Don, Larrikin Entertainment & our audience.

Equipment acknowledgments to: Geoff Deerling for Carl Thompson Bass Strings, Jeff Mallia - Mallia Basses, Sabian Cymbals & Sleishman Drums.

Tracks 3,4,5,9 Studio X (Mark Don)
Other Tracks Paradise Studios (Alex Wong)

Steve Hunter © Control.
Tracks 1, 2, 4, 7, 9 Copyright Guy Leclaire/ Leclairevoyeurnt Tunes./ PFP Music.

John Foreman appears courtesy of BMG Records

Photos by **Michelle Darlington, Mary Szental, Wendy McDougall, Peter Rosetzy**

Sleeve Design by **Cameron Moss/Serious Business**

This album is dedicated to our children, Isabel, Julien, Louis & Nastassja

Correspondence to **PLAYDIEM**
P.O Box 683 Glebe NSW 2037 Australia

When four of Australia's most impressive jazz musicians get to play together the audience can certainly expect the unexpected and that's exactly what **PLAYDIEM** deliver! The music on this album is refreshingly innovative (they're all originals) and further evidence that Australian jazz musicians can stand tall with the rest of the world and even deliver music that stands taller!! Guy Le Claire and Steve Hunter are both acknowledged as leading stylists of the guitar and bass respectively whilst David Jones has often been described as 'the drummers drummer' and John Foreman, although a recent graduate from the Sydney Conservatorium on Music, is already recognised as one of the country's leading pianist. It wouldn't be an understatement (or record company hype) to say that this recording is chock full of real music and great music at that.
Warren Fahey

We formed, so Steve and I got to work on putting out an original CD. With mates rates through A.I.M. We recorded at Paradise studios with engineer Alex Fong (what a blast it was), and Larrikin Records agreed to release it. this is what Warren Fahey(President of Larrikin Records and Folkways) had to say .

I played my Ibanez RG 550 through my marshall JMP-1 to Sovtek Quad, I had a digitech deal and was running all manner of rack mounts with a midi foot controller. Live the band was super powerful, and once Steve and David got on a roll, it was like a pride of lions charging right up me ass. John was like an angel, bringing in light and shade at essential moments.

Colin asked 'if I wanna play dat music do I have to practise 10 hours a day?'. I replied who'd wanna play yit anyway?

MATT FINISH 1990 & 2008

With the introduction of more sophisticated chords, propagated by the great Andy Summers (the Police), still pretty much following the standard forms of I IV V or blues progs. guitarists were restructuring the sounds by adding 9ths or 11ths or as in Short Note Dmaj9 to Amaj9(the difference is thus see below) Matt Finish presented me with a very challenging task, unusual chords and rhythms. Lindsay Jehan (bassist - Euroz) and I became something of a hired duo, freelancing with Rick Price, Troy Newman, Shauna Jensen, and with Troy we were introduced to the world of John Prior, drum man for Matt Finish and bandleader plus studio session ace.1989 Matt Moffatt was eager to get back out on the road, and John plonked Lindsay and me into the band, along with Jenny from NYC. I played the rg550(a tele woulda been better) and me cantankerous Red nosed Twin. We did our homework (true pros) and even Matt mentioned he felt Lindz and I knew the songs better than he did! Guy Le Claire – guitar (1990–1993, 2008, 2012)

We played Sydney, Melbourne and others in 1989-90. with Matt's unpredictable behaviour the band fizzled out. In 2008 a second incarnation evolved with Dave Adams singing (RIP Matt) and Harry Brus on bass, I rejoined for a NSW tour. It was a pleasure working with these gentlemen, however health wise I was unwell. I played Ben Li's '75 strat through Dikran Balian's loaned Mesa Boogie. On the last tour with Harry Brus (bass), John Prior (drums), David Adams (vocal/guitar), guesting Dale Barlow (saxes) and Kevin Borich, I fell sick and needed medical attention, retreating back to my crib in Hong Kong. All touring for me stopped. No More touring Are We There Yets.

No More Blues…

I'm going back home

I promise no more to roam

Home is where the heart is

The fun the parties

My hearts been right there all along

No more fears

And no more sighs

No more tears

I've said my last good-byes

If trouble beckons me I swear I'm going to refuse

No more Blues – Jobim/Jon Hendricks

FREELANCING 1980 to 2014

The Guitar world involves many styles from fingerpicking country style to MOR pop to Rock /prog rock incorporating various sounds and effects, to Bossa and delicate nylon string parts, Classical to Jazz and all it's genres.

The task faced by a session guitarist is daunting. One can be a jack of all trades but often - a master of none. Raising one's hand to sessions requires latest gear and versatility along with experience and listening skills, not to mention the ability to sight read music and follow charts!

You can't just act through it because your footprint is being documented on a recording. You may get away with it for a time. The ability to hear, listen and analyse then make quick creative, relatable judgement and to proceed with your part willfully contributing to the recording project that hopefully your employer will dig!

It is demanding work!

My downfall in the studio was my hearing defect, however as a leader I surrounded myself with close allies/engineers/musicians along with an abundance of energy, determination and direction. I managed to document most of my own projects. Belief in oneself is essential.

I freelanced for Nic Clarke, Shauna Jensen, Sam McNally, Rick Price, Mark Williams, Rated X, Kamahl, Mark Riley, Martha Reeves, BJ Thomas, Brickhouse - Ronald La Prea, Revolution, Howard McCrary, Justin Siu, Troy Newman, Deanie Yip, George Lam, Sally Yeh, Tsai Tsin, Faye Wong. Tommy E, Toni Mott, Paul Najar, Tamar, Tania Bower.

TOURING:

what goes on on the road, stays on the road!

'on the road again, just can't wait to get on the road again'

Phil Witchet " pilots are just glorified bus drivers", Bell's father said "stewardesses are glorified waitresses"

Touring is an endless question of "Are we there yet?" it also involves very not glorified moments of emotional trauma and frustration. Long periods away from family & loved ones, inability to lead a somewhat normal human existence. Man was made to hunt, sow daytime, eat dinner sleep night-time to replenish. Sleep patterns are drastically disturbed. Touring fucks all that up! Musoz are not the only one's touring, there are many other industries reliant on touring.

Upon arrival at the gig on the tour it is essential to do a Sound Check, make sure your rigs are functioning properly and the PA is working /mixes in order. because after overcoming your nerves, gaining your confidence to hit the stage and start the show. There is nothing worse than gear breaking down/malfunctioning, out of tune guitars!!! mix fucked up by some fucker!

There is nothing better than being part of a great performance/show. Art is YinYang friends!

The show has to work, so the moment you begin it all starts flowing and as Kenny Werner says, you can get into the Zone!

A Good show /performance is the biggest and best buzz! Ever!

That's why we tour and tour, and wonder Are we there yet?

More...

BRUCE CALE AND GUY LE CLAIRE DUO1985-6

Lars Knudsen, a deep family friend had a beautiful property in Hampton on the Jenolan Caves Rd., His neighbours were Bruce and Pat Cale, Lars was having a party and invited me. I appeared, I had my guitar and amp in the boot, Bruce was playing his upright bass, so I joined in. Of course I had heard of Bruce, he is an Oz jazz legend, and exponent of George Russell's Lydian Chromatic Concept which intrigued me. He had formed a number of ensembles, since coming back to Oz to live, after a good long period of living in the UK and USA. Bruce Cale Orchestra (Basement) stood as a pinnacle in Aussie Jazz featuring the top young players and Bruce's compositions!

Playing my JB strat through a little peavey, Bruce and I hit it off. I was seriously intrigued and wanted to spend more time with this gentleman. I would wake up and dive into Bondi beach waters, then hop into my Citroen and drive through the blue mountains ascend the Jenolan road to Bruce's once a week on my day off. We played and Bruce guided me with Lydian Chromatic tonal concept of Organisation and tackling Jazz standards. I ended up living back in the mountains which enabled us to perform every weekend (Fri-Sat) at the Hillcrest Coachman (now the Bunker), it was a wonderful period for both of us that lasted two years, until the sways of partners ended it.

Are we there yet? DETOUR AHEAD:. 1996 on

The ole Hong Kong - multiple screen roles and stages

the 3 $'s $oke $unts & $ash.

Hong Kong's music scene originally was influenced by cinema, latin-tangos cha cha, big bands. Most of HK's movers and shakers escaped Shanghai and the communist regime. It was known that Shanghai had a large film/entertainment industry as HK inherited it. Later in the 1960s when US/AUS soldiers took RNR in HK from the Vietnam war, they hung around red light district Wanchai, all the little girlie bars had live bands, the places were run by the Triads booking local musicians and singers (cheaper) and through the apprenticeship of this era the musicians and businessmen gained experienced. At the end of the war a lot of those 'local' musicians became the faces for a new popular genre known as 'Cantopop".

When I arrived in 1979 the scene was predominantly Filipino, with Tony Carpio sitting at the top. A great musician and guitarist, Tony held a regular Sunday slot at the Excelsior Hotel, we all flocked there. There was Ned Kelly's Jazz pub, with Benny on tpt. And Cocktails in TST that was about it.

However, in the interim years I had been away (about 15 years) things changed dramatically. When I went back in 1996 it was a mix of local Chinese, Philippines, Americans with a good number of Black Americans. The Grand Hyatt HK was importing black funk/dance bands by Sheraton Carter into it's hip swanky club. The bands proved super popular, with a lot of the band members loving HK, so they stayed and the local music population was sprinkled with these fine musicians, bringing their music and culture into the scene. I was recruited into it, another movie and role to wallow around in. It was super exciting as I got to play the classic soul/funk repertoire.

Not only was I in a movie here, but I was the director! I could rock up anywhere and go into a role that I saw fit, a true hypocrite Actor. and I got working heaps! needed some juice most times.

"Enter the Poc Guy" my ultimate movie!

Hong Kong had a good amount of guitarists too:

Eugene Pao - a Master, Skip Moy, Tommy Ho, Miguel, Cary Abrahams, Kevin Duffy, David Tong, Ron Ng, Teriver Cheung, Dodong, Joey Villanueva and of course the great Tony Carpio, Greg Chako, Ivan Grand Solberg, Derick Sepnio, ABA, A dude from Houston who flipped his guitar left hander played awesomely!, Anthony Bautista, Jason Ho and Karissa Muse, Philip Penfold, Quincy Aranas, Balu Casi, Mano Manok, Chris the solicitor, Pak Yip Cheng, Jason Ho, Chris Collins. Greg Chako, Dodong Fuego.

Hong Kong was also a place where one could while away practice hours (when you had time- time being a valuable commodity up there), inspired by the local musicians!

I'd like to also thank Peter Lee (organiser tour promoter), Anthony Fernandes (hk's great drummer), Paul Candelaria, Eugene Pao, Peter Scherr, Allen Youngblood, Blaine Whittaker, Elaine Liu, Bin Bin McPhee, Sylvain Gagnon, Mano Manolette, Mark Henderson, Guy Le Claire, Mark Peter, Larry Hammond, Rickard Malmsten, Flynn & Robbin - and all my Chinese Kung Fu Masters shakers and movers up there!

With Elaine we first played as a duo (vocal/guitar) at the Bruce Lee Cafe, Mid-levels, owned by Jon Benn the dude who played the Italian mafia boss in "Way of the Dragon".

Playing duo with a fine passionate singer focussing on the great American songbook, expanded my jazz knowledge and ability. We settled on a regular Tuesday night for 2 years in Stauntons Bar (Kim yay)

9//11: I was on stage with Larry Hammond (drums) & Paul Candelaria (bass), backing a US black blues artist from Philly at the Jazz Club, when

Larry's phone rang and he answered in the middle of the performance! We all looked at him in disbelief, later he said he only answers that number in severe emergency. Anyway, his face on answering went ashen as he hopped off the drums to announce a cuppla planes had gone into the twin towers NYC. We all left the stage and went to the bar which had a tv and watched in disbelief this most disgusting scenario.

* * *

In 2004 I got the job of jazz band-leader for the "Venetian"(Macau) the biggest Casino in the world (Sheldon Adelson's crib).

I flew in Chris Cuzme NYC, Wayne from Canberra and Nicholas McBride & Scott Dodd from Shanghai. Arriving in Macau myself from Adelaide with boxes of charts and stuff from my Sai Kung country park crib I was ready to conquer the world. We got started, placed in the high rollers room with a manager that disliked jazz and preferred Country music. The pressure escalated with me called in daily by the management for appraisals and stress. I hadn't worked for an American organisation before. It was a fucken pain in the arse! What a dump! The dutyfree bottle O became my best friend- As well as after gig antics with the band at "The Monkey Bar" The music making environment proved too much for this little guy, so I quit after 3 months, retreating back to my Sai kung crib, with daily trips to beautiful Hoi Ha beach to nurse myself back to health. throughout this I played my beloved Gibbo 175.

* * *

"Funff" got 1st class on the jetfoil to go over to Beihai, China, it was friggin funny sitting up there on the top deck with Blaine, Robbin & Seb. I was playing my inherited strat. As my teaching biz blossomed in Clearwater Bay, I got a message from Oz key whiz Rick Mellick, who was touring internationally with Joe Bonamassa, about 50 tickets to the HK show were organized by Rick(thx man),I took all my young hk students to the show, we had the best time! thank you Rick!

Back to the China gig - the crowd really dug us, with rock star like treatment after signing copies of the posters /CDs etc. The area we played in was a reconstructed old farmhouse. just across the hk border.

With land and space the mainlanders were creating intense admirable venues and villages. Yangshuo being one.

* * *

When i left Adelaide (2020) to come back to the Blue Mountains, I took the same route as Bell and I had done before out of Ado, pass the silos, the maccas where we booked our hotel room - didn't know if we would hook up again. Stayed in Ballarat, a beautiful town that reminded me of Guangzhou. Paid high respects to the Eureka Stockade location. after a few days there, pushed off for a days drive to Lithgow where my son was. Leaving at 4am in the dark, I reached Daylesford in a misty pre-dawn dream, narrowly missed 2 big dopey grey kangaroos, reaching Tocumwal on the border, and in NSW away from Covid was reassuring, chilled out down by the Murray river, still about another 8 hours to go I pushed off , this time not in a Commodore but the trusted Mitsubishi 380 - 3.8 V6 made in ado. Towards Bathurst, a really beautiful drive. Lithgow appeared, comfy for the night in my son's hotel room.

* * *

BLACK MUSIC IN OZ RESTRICTIONS

SOUL MUSIC

R&B soul music had a significant impact on Australia's music, although it is notable that many seminal recordings in this genre by American acts of the late 20th century were not played on Australian radio. Anecdotal evidence suggest that racism was a key factor—in his book on the history of Australian radio, author and broadcaster Wayne Mac recounts that when a local Melbourne DJ of the 1960s played the new Ike and Tina Turner single "River Deep Mountain High" it was immediately pulled from the playlist by the station's program manager for being "too noisy and too black".[19] As a result, many local soul/R&B hits of this period were cover versions recorded by Australian acts. Despite radio's reluctance to play American soul/R&B originals, these styles were avidly adopted by local performers and covers of soul/R&B standards were staples in the setlists of many acts including Max Merritt and the Meteors, Doug Parkinson, Jeff St John, The Groop, The Groove, The Twilights, Renee Geyer and many others.

Renée Geyer is an Australian singer who came to prominence in the mid-1970s, has long been regarded as one of the finest exponents of jazz, soul and R&B idioms. She had commercial success as a solo artist in Australia, with "It's a Man's Man's World "Rock historian, Ian McFarlane described her as having a "rich, soulful, passionate and husky vocal delivery". Geyer's iconic status in the Australian music industry was recognised when she was inducted into the ARIA Hall of Fame on 14 July 2005.

theory shit...

TWO WAY!

SOME HARMONIC (CHORD) CONSIDERATIONS:

Coltrane Matrix – get on a train the major 3rd train rails. Rayalls Rayalls.C, E. G#, c, e, g#, repeat until you arrive at gare du nord!

Triads – another rayall 1. Up major 3rd, up minor 3rd, up perfect 4th, start again and again = Major/ 2. Up minor 3rd, up major 3rd, up a perfect 4th, start again = Minor Triad

CHROMATICISM:Chromo

FLOURISHED IN THE WEST AS THE WORLD SUFFERED 2 WORLD WARS AND UNTOLD GRIEF, THE CHROMO ENABLED MUSIC TO PULL AWAY FROM TONALITY AND FOLK MUSIC, PAVING A NEW WAY FORWARDING A NEW REALM JUST LIKE THE WORLD & SOCIETY.

THIS GRAVITATIONAL societal pull left out the indigenous rhythms that had been developed over the centuries by indigenous tribes.

Chromaticism is a compositional technique interspersing the primary diatonic pitches and chords with other pitches of the chromatic scale. Chromaticism is in contrast or addition to tonality or diatonicism and modality (the major and minor, or "white key", scales). Chromatic elements are considered, "elaborations of or substitutions for diatonic scale members".

"Not only at the beginning of a composition but also in the midst of it, each scale-step [degree] manifests an irresistible urge to attain the value of the tonic for itself as that of the strongest scale-step. If the composer yields to this urge of the scale-step within the diatonic system of which this scale-step forms part, I call this process tonicalization and the phenomenon itself chromatic."

— Heinrich Schenker (1906)

"Chromaticism is almost by definition an alteration of, an interpolation in or deviation from this basic diatonic organization."

— Leonard B. Meyer (1956)

"Throughout the nineteenth century, composers felt free to alter any or all chord members of a given tertian structure [chord built from thirds] according to their compositional needs and dictates. Pronounced or continuous chordal alteration [and 'extension'] resulted in chromaticism. Chromaticism, together with frequent modulations and an abundance of non-harmonicism [non-chord tones], initially effected an expansion of the tertian system; the overuse of the procedures late in the century forewarned the decline and near collapse [atonality] of the system [tonality]."

— Paul Cooper (1975)

"Chromaticism is the name given to the use of tones outside the major or minor scales. Chromatic tones began to appear in music long before the common-practice period, and by the beginning of that period were an important part of its melodic and harmonic resources. Chromatic tones arise in music partly from inflection [alteration] of scale degrees in the major and minor modes, partly from secondary dominant harmony, from a special vocabulary of altered chords, and from certain nonharmonic tones... Notes outside the scale do not necessarily affect the tonality...tonality is established by the progression of roots and the tonal functions of the chords, even though the details of the music may contain all the tones of the chromatic scale."

— Walter Piston (1987)

"Sometimes...a melody based on a regular diatonic scale (major or minor) is laced with many accidentals, and although all 12 tones of the chromatic scale may appear, the tonal characteristics of the diatonic scale are maintained. Chromaticism is the introduction of some pitches of the chromatic scale into music that is basically diatonic in orientation, or music that is based on the chromatic scale instead of the diatonic scales."

— Benward & Saker (2003)

* * *

Ritual, Religious song/chanting music:

the instruments could represent the sounds of the weather and animals + human voices. Nature sounds/sound physics.

knowing this and that, is good for this and that, maybe intellectually satisfying, spontaneity is good for a time, then 1 must overcome it.

knowing how to do something & doing it is far better than dissecting it intellectually in constipated non activity. Just do it.

Old Willy 'the Taoist'.

THE MAN WHO PLANNED EVERYTHING.

The man who planned everything was able to visualise his whole days, hour by hour. I will do this and that, the outcome will result in that and this, and so it went, until one day nothing turned out right!!! then what!!!???this fellow was in a pickle, everything planned calculated amounted to the wrong outcome. How could it be!!!???

gau chor a!!!!

THE COUPLE WHO HAD EVERYTHING

This couple had a car, a house, a baby, food on the table what more could they possibly want?

LIVING BY IMPULSES:

Be empty my friends.

THE VOICE OR VOCAL

Voice or vocal is the fundamental expression of human. I believe in my older age now, it is imperative for a musician to get in touch with his voice. Here's a quote from wikipedia (whom I think needs our support) 'The human voice consists of sound made by a human being using the vocal tract, including talking, singing, laughing, crying, screaming, shouting, humming or yelling. The human voice frequency is specifically a part of human sound production in which the vocal folds (vocal cords) are the primary sound source. (Other sound production mechanisms produced from the same general area of the body involve the production of unvoiced consonants, clicks, whistling and whispering.)The vocal folds, in combination with the articulators, are capable of producing highly intricate arrays of sound.[2][3][4] The tone of voice may be modulated to suggest emotions such as anger, surprise, fear, happiness or sadness. The human voice is used to express emotion,[5] and can also reveal the age and sex of the speaker.[6][7][8] Singers use the human voice as an instrument for creating music.[9]'

The rejection of the voice referendum for an indigenous voice to parliament for Australian Aboriginal & Torres Strait Islanders by the people in Australia is very disappointing.

George Benson Bop scattered with his guitar, along w Shawn Lane inspired by Nasrat Inayat Khan.

Peace!

CHINESE KUNG FU IS AN AMAZING INVENTION...

PERSONALLY I WAS TRAINED IN WING CHUN BY SIFU PO KIN WAH IN HK. I LOVED THE CENTRE STRAIGHT LINE AND USE OF BIO MECHANIC IN DEFELECTING/ATTACKING, ADDITIONALLY I SPENT 3 YEARS IN CHINA PARTICIPATING IN CHEN SHI TAI JI, LOCAL FOLK ART BUDHIZHEN AND QI GONG, AS WELL AS PURSUING IT ALL IN HK TO RECOVER FROM STROKE.

INCREDIBLE EXPERIENCE BEING AWARE OF DIRECT LINES AND CIRCULAR MOVEMENT. ABSOLUTELY LOVE IT!

Left turn ahead AIRPORT

Hong Kong 1979 to 2015

Mr Dale Wilson Sifu, I met Dale (the son of Cantonese speaking Mr & Mrs Wilson - American Baptist missionaries)

In 1979 while living on Lamma Island HK.

Dale played piano and had been to North Texas State. Besides being a gifted musician, he introduced me to Steely Dan, Burt Bacharach and Tony Bennet, we along with my Mum and the Derricks were the first Westerners to inhabit Lamma Island – a cute natural 'outlying island' 45 minutes by ferry from overwhelming, exciting, chaotic Downtown HK. The near 2 years I lived there was euphoric. Later, by about 20 years, Dale secured music professor status (ethnomusicologist) at Columbia U/ NYC. He periodically appeared back in HK to research Chinese folk music, namely in Toishan, Guangdong Prov. Where he said existed in a near fossilised state ethnic ritual music practices. Once a HK friend (photographer – John) told me Chinese Blues music comes from Toishan.

Hong Kong Stories cont':

HKU had an adventurous head of Music Department - Australian Dr Mano Manolette. Mano and I bonded, he formed "Afro-Cuba" with Mark Henderson and we gigged much as the Cuban craze gripped HK, in addition Mano was running the HKU Gamelan orchestra, and commissioned Gerard Brophy to compose a gamelan piece which featured electric guitar and subsequently myself. Trying to contribute to such an ensemble was challenging as gamelan tuning can be a challenge in itself, as well as choosing the right sound to sit in the sonic mix. Mano's visions enabled me to get involved and perform with many wonderful musicians i.e. Adrian McNeil (Dr and sarod master), Theremin exponent -Eric Ross. Digital Cut up Lounge – John Von Seggern & Stephen Ives.

He also introduced us to Professor Wayne Cristaudo on the uni faculty from Adelaide, a deep thinker, published author and songwriter, who was produced by Peter Scherr allowing me to rampage all manner of guitar on his debut album.

HK session ace for a minute, included backing Martha Reeves and BJ Thomas(raindrops keep falling on my head) in huge auditoriums but the best time I had was with brick house Ronald La Preau in a really small club with Robbin & JezReal. Faye Wong TV performance what an arvo!

Not to mention all the blues cats from the US at jazz club. and the

Aussies jazz.

TURN RIGHT AIRPORT Ahead

Landing in Mumbai, India in 1999, exposed a large amount of banknotes to a rather small amount of $$ in the Airport money exchange. The cab driver was a prick driving all over the place, then picking up some guy, I smelt a rat, and exclaimed I had the best kung fu ever, a gun in my coat as my hand became a gun in his rear vision mirror I became 007. Getting to my hotel near Leo's, I took off to get a beer., Leos shut, everywhere shut, I didn't know I was just behind the Taj Mahal hotel, some bloke took me to a place with big heavy doors,

I asked can I get a beer? The door guy let me in arriving with beer I sat downstairs slugging and heard loud music emanating from upstairs, asked can I go up there? Yes, went in, Indian chicks were dancing around to bollywood beats in saris while blokes were throwing bank notes at them, I settled down to the strangest movie, acting like Sean Connery, the bloke next to me was throwing de money & said "Oh Australian… Love Australia"-play Bond theme in yo head. I managed about an hour in there, after inspecting the local ladies, then clambered to bed in my new hotel, waking to the magnificence of life in Mumbai.

The Vrindaban HK Association had set up this trip, and it was hoped that I would have some session/lessons with Hariprasad Chaurasia, as he was on the road… are you there yet. I was relegated to Rakesh Chaurasia (nephew) and an informative session was had and enjoyed, coincidentally there was an Indian Classical Music festival on, and I fortunately got to see/hear the top performers. Finally, I contacted Louis Banks (India's father of jazz), and with his generous invite, I had a sumptuous lunch at his place with his wife, Sivamani (notable percussionist) and an Afro-American singer, who was fulfilling a contract at one of the swanky hotels. My short time in India was extraordinary.

Hong Kong had a lot of musical employment opportunities, if one was skilled & able to cut it (cutting it is not just being able to play, but also being able to listen, comply & 'get along' – watch ya ego!) HK is fast & pushy, Shanghai, more lilting seemed to attract jazz cats that were studious, dedicated, the jazz produced there differed. Beijing seemed to be more 'indie' music rock vibe, both shaghai and b jing utilised Chinese & ethnic music.

Top performances attended:

KERALA TEMPLE DRUMMERS -the father explained he beats a simple 1234. beginning slowly and nods to the other drummers in the circular line standing ensemble to join him in rhythm, by the time they all are playing the rhythm - he either a) doubles it in duple time or b) does in triple time. The tempo may increase but subtly. The effect at the concert resulted in a sound that I thought resembles an Alien language it was incredible and it was only drums! Seriously like other being talking & I wasn't stoned.

JOE HENDERSON – darn that was good

JOSHUA REDMAN 4TH DIMENSION – dug the way Josh presented himself and his music. Thoughtful stage set-up and real music.

JOHN Williams SLAVA Grigoryan – good but forgot what they played oh well. Perhaps it was 2 separate occasions. Me thinks.

CHINESE ETHNIC MUSIC

I had been captivated by the ethnic music in China. Provincial music from Xinjiang, Mongolia and Yunnnan fascinated me. I attended concerts by the HK Chinese Orchestra, & collaborated with Erhu player TomTse, eventually attending a new world music seminar in Shanghai. Also lived in SW China for over a year in the ethnic area.

In HK we also had the Brazilian cats, Joao Mascarenhas, Sergio Brandao, Paulo Levi bringing their music locally, HK simply was a very exciting place to be in. These cats introduced beyond the beautiful Jobim et al Bossa Novas to Hermeto Pasqual & contemporary Brazz Jazz.

There were a vast array of characters in HK, with lots of roles to choose from.

I had finally arrived at my ideal rig in about 2012

1.D'Angelico Excel guitar playing through my

2. Hughes & Kettner amp head into a Hughes&Kettner small 15 cab running lots of

3. boutique pedals on a ready-made board, like "Freeze", "Looper"MXR delay, Line6 green thingo. big muff, mxr carbon copy and reverb, tc elec ditto looper,Boss pitch shifter Harmonist.el har old glove, holy grail.

In addition I had Ben's CBS strat, theRG 550, a Martin hecho en Mexico acoustic and the startling Kif hybrid acoustic /rope core strings. All was lost or sold when I got sick.

Hong Kong enabled me to make a decent living as a mainly jazz improvising guitarist. It was a great scene for a while there.

Samantha Vogee a resourceful hard working ex-pat Aussie now ex-HKer, who worked for David - an events initiator/co-ordinator, Sam masterminded the "history of Rock" a show she put together to educate school kids on Rock. Franklin Torres - bass, Jezreal Lucero - keys, brother Robbin -drums and I were put together - The Band to back up the super talented young British acting/singing/dancing cast . spanning from RocknRoll, de Beatles, Queen, Pink etc. we fucking killed it. The school kids would go wild! Dancing, rollicking until the Front of House columns nearly came tumbling down - kids on stage everywhere all in a lost frenzy! We were able to act as 'rock stars'.

This gig allowed some of us to do perhaps another 2 gigs that day as this show was mostly mornings. (most schools in Asia have two sessions - morning sesh the smart ones and arvo sesh). Me and Robbin often trundled off later to two more gigs. It was a busy time, potentially messing with the mind in a fantasy of fame etc.

Acting can be a strange zone as one then re-enters 'their' self role. After sesh.

The guitar fretboard is the universe, displaying all manner of interpretations and possibilities - it is yin and yang. real kung fu- if you get it right you become master and may have a fulfilling career what about the piano? what an instrument so beautiful!

I used my music theory etc. to make critical judgements, as I was part deaf. If I couldn't quite 'hear it' I had my theory backup systems – didn't always work. Possibly not the best way to do things, although in older age I find me backup systems useful, advantageous.

Peter Scherr's "Blue" album & project was a mind expanding experience, Coupled with Peter's genius was Matt McMahon – piano, Bruce Huron – sax, Simon Barker – drums & me.

* * *

Biomechanics:

the study of human movement including the interaction between the participant and equipment. Primarily these studies are broken down into two broad areas: kinetics (the study of forces acting on the body) and kinematics (the study of movements of the body). I believe the understanding of this interaction the musician is doing, to be of great value, be aware: your posture, your muscles, your tenseness, your fingerings.

Memories…

MUSIC: CHINA

Shanghai housed the knowledgable jazz cats

Beijing was indie rocksville

MEXICO1976:

Settling in San Miguel de Allende with Mum, exposed a whole new world for this little Mosmanite, we lived in cute Mexican village houses, I met Max y Charlie eating tortillas daily, met many young Americans who were studying at the fine arts school, which upon graduation their degree was recognised back home. A cheap exciting location to study and get qualified. I myself was at the local government Belles Artes (fine arts school). My main focus was on guitar, and Pedro my rotund teacher sat in a huge cavernous room with his classical guitar, music stand and spittoon, he only spoke Spanish and spat frequently into the spittoon.

He would send me home to practise, but I didn't know what the key signatures were with the sharps and flats plus my Spanish wasn't so hot, I would confidently recite my homework first, minus the altered notes, then

Pedro would play the piece in the key of A piece after me with its 3 sharps, and I would sit there baffled. This went on for a while until I figured it out.

Anyway, San Miguel a beautiful Mexican historical town located about 250 miles North-West of Mexico City in Guanajuato state. Everyday, for the year I was there, it was ritual to 'hang' in the zocalo/ el jardim

(town square). Mexican life was vastly different to back home. Festivals included "Day of the Dead" with other events combining strong religious activity & art things. The Mexican artists were divine.

USA

CALIFORNIA 1977: then 2006

I loved California, I had my 17th birthday in San Fran, with Mum as we lived with Andre and his Mum in Corte Madera, Andre used to drag me along to his school, I was popular especially when I spoke, later in 2006, Mum and I flew into LA on our way back to Mexico where we had lived arriving stuffed from Tokyo, we got to our LA motel Mum had a lie down & I went straight to the legendary Musicians Institute, a trippy tour guide around the faculty enlivened my appreciation for LA.

I was not there like Barnesy to record or crack big-time, coming away disappointed and disliking the place. I Loved it, hung one day with Mr. Frank Gambale at his crib in the hills. I also bought my JB strat on Sunset boulevard.

NYC:Australian Lindsay Jehan a total professional with a strong work ethic. Had a gig(Producer/Engineer/Composer) and leverage working for Baron & Baron (NYC). Arriving from HK I am staying with Lindz in his loft apartment- Spring St., stuffed, I sleep, up next morning and dragged into Lindz studio I found myself recording/sessioning all manner of music. 5 days a week. David Wilson also worked there, recommending me to stay on as I had the knack to cover most styles needed, donning my by now expert acting roles, I was able to drop most stuff they needed jingles whereas previously they had to get a rock, or a latin, or a jazz expert in pending the style of music. But I was like the Burger with the works - a deal was done, whereby the studio would mix/master my latest CD " On the One"

https://guyleclaire.bandcamp.com/album/on-the-one

and Lindz would put me up.

I don't USA to get in. I observed the well-off young jazzers mostly Jewish surnames, well- educated and trained, twisting jazz music to a private language, like a fucken club, with doormen to bar entree. Fuck that! It was for me funny in the older days when some jazz cat would declare that they spent time in NYC. "So What" as Miles said… go to Mumbai and Paris to get the feel of life to get the … of life from Jazz and Cocktails". I preferred the gritty, rough organic side of life and opportunity in HK. No desire me stay like a wetback. So I was glad when I could return to HK. For me HK is way more exciting than NYC!

At least I got to attend Elvin Jones birthday bash and meet Him at blue note, also saw Pat Martino,

Zinc bar - Ron Affif, Jeff Tain Watts, James Genus, Dave Kikowski and Mark Whitfield, Richie Beirach, Smalls, Bar 55. walking around a small supermarket I come across Willem De Foe reciting lines to himself, left him alone. We all actors! I went hard in NYC.

FRANCE:

taking off from Charles Kingsford Smith in 1974 with Dad was beyond exciting. We picked up our rented Renault 4 and hit the fertile Loire Valley - where I pooped from a hole down the cliff. Everything was new and different. stopping at the north of Marseilles we had Aioli for the 1st time. driving through Cannes I expected to see Brigitte Bardot or that French singer/guitarist.

CHINA 2003

I'm a sinophile , and I can say Chinese people love Music!. One can witness their emotions when listening and participating in Music. It's awesome really.

The ethnic musics of China offer as much as a tantalising adventure as the Provinces it comes from - Yunnan, Guangxi (where I lived), Guizhou, Gansu, Xinjiang, Sichuan and Mongolia. Han Hong melts my heart!

SHANGHAI: Based in the Shanghai Conservatory of Music in the French Concessioner Huai Zhong Lu(st.), I walked miles and miles fascinated, exploring.um um...

JAPAN

don't know much about Japan people assume I do as I am part Chinese.

*　*　*

BANFF, CANADA- 2001/2002

I managed two trips to the Banff Centre for the Arts, Calgary, Alberta, Canada. The first time I was to attend their contemporary jazz program run by Kenny Werner, (previously by Dave Holland, Oscar Peterson, Phil Woods) and I must say living/sharing with Jim Black, Dave Douglas, Joe Lovano and Judi Silvano was a great experience, being able to sit with these masters in the dining room or cafe & listen/chat. Sadly my Dad passed on in Katoomba on the 1st day, affecting my being big time. To deal with Dad's passing, I would go on long bike rides through the Rockies. Shit scared of bears, I would pant through dark passageways, to then view a most beautiful vista and take a pic. Some people mistakenly thought I was out having a good time while Dad lay in a fridge, this was my way of dealing with it. Getting Back to Nature. From this first time 'Six To Go' was formed with Michael Bates, Joe Sorbaro, Cindy Fairbanks - Canada and Peter Knight, Fiona Burnett, plus myself - Australia. We received Artist in Residence scholarship to return a second time about a year later. We composed some great music and got it all recorded in the Centre's Sound Studio.

Alex Tsiboulski from Adelaide was there also, a brilliant classical guitarist, his Brouwer pieces knocked me out.

Still in an Alien Spaceship

disability is a new venture in my life. I still have logic to make reasonable judgement I think thank God, and I seriously want to thank all Australians that work their arses off to pay tax etc. and whose judgement and continued support for those that can't work are able to receive invalid pensions etc. it's a tough world but the ones that support social services are definitely my heroes!

Brett Morris retired from nrl, as injuries forced his hand ,and he accepts this scenario. Fuck musoz injuries force their hand, as it did for me..this morning i played tai chi quan on my kung fu veranda in the awesome winter sun, and realised this is it!

There has been no improvement plus I played guitar for a while and everything is just the same as when i got sick 10 years ago. from a psychological point of view /one can internally talk but the western doctor/medicine are correct.

darn.

CONTROL:

it could be that corona virus and strains is a government invention and permutation suggested by lord aliens as a method to control the population. what better way to get control insert a needle of unknown stuff into just about every living human being/trace it/condition it/possibly alter the vac contents/kill it. Control.

Slow Down:

"There must be some way out of here"

Said the joker to the thief

"There's too much confusion

I can't get no relief

Businessmen, they drink my wine

Plowmen dig my earth

None of them along the line

Know what any of it is worth"

"No reason to get excited"

The thief, he kindly spoke

"There are many here among us

Who feel that life is but a joke

But you and I, we've been through that

And this is not our fate

So let us not talk falsely now

The hour is getting late"

All along the watchtower

Princes kept the view

While all the women came and went

Barefoot servants too

Outside, in the distance

A wildcat did growl

Two riders were approaching

The wind began to howl.

Bob Dylan.

gates of the Philistines. The hill I

* * *

Gear used on my recordings:

Trio at Jazz club - Gibson 175 through the house Fender Deville great amp.

Trio 2 - through my Hughes and Kettner on a D"Angelico excel DC.

Solo 1 & 2 on my custom-built, ordered by Esteban Antonio KIF (Cornwall) Acoustic – rope core strings thanks Thomastik-Infeld!

My Ibanez Rg rg550 was retired and i passed it onto student Luke Riggs, the ibanez I used on all my early recordings. Storage, Lost my Mexican made Martin acoustic I adored.

ITS NOT EASY BEING AN EXPAT:

the stress of it all made me sick.

Expleted all my energy, flying up and down, sick father in a nursing home, kids growing up in a foreign environment, dealing with foreign concepts and language - it's not easy, it wasn't easy, it was easier to just work hard, get money, and get out of it, big time!!!

I just attended the world's largest CPR class on tv, it was good

16th Oct. '21.

FB I have formed a band with South African Willem Van Der Merwe, along with Chris Collins, brother Robbin Harris & Brit Roger. I play bass & guitar swapping with Chris, had a ball, dyed my hair blond thinking I am Flea! Oh the roles keep 'em coming… are we there yet?

Tonal Colours/Settings

Pat Metheny an incredibly accomplished guitarist with a distinctive voice, introduced Brazilian instruments/sounds and vocal expression

be aware:

Syncopation

Keys

Transposition

Tempo

Intervals

Transcribing

Scores/Charts etc.

on the Gig

Professionalism

Ego 'We were all " young and pretty once" Ego is something any artist can relate to, particularly if you're involved in an image conscious biz like ours. I won't lie as my students have always been well aware of my favourite

Wadsworth pearl of wisdom. " Ya gotta earn your haircut" meaning ' You can look the part, but if ya can't cut it on stage or in the studio' ya gonna look like a right plonker!' now I'm older and happily embracing my Richardesque head, I still endeavour to keep a reasonable playing level everytime I sit at the kit. If I dont' I'm finished.

To my dear young friends " have a blast" I did. X'

Tubby Wadsworth.

"We don't spend our lives devoted to learning about harmony, learning about melody, learning to master our instruments, learning our instruments, to stop there. I tell people that what they need to do is make that next step. To go from the level of improvisers to the level of artists who have something unique, who can come up with melodies of their own. In that sense, we have to get away from the world of the guitar, the world of guitar players and into the realm of sound, of music, of developing strong melodies, of being able to say things, of being able to phrase, which is a challenge for guitar players."
Joshua Breakstone

STUDIO WORK:

Peter Cobbin Studios 301. this sort of work can possibly be the most challenging…trying to interpret the artist's musical vision - and recording or "laying tracks" that are satisfactory.

Not to mention keeping unto date with the latest sounds and "gizmos". Or sight-reading skills. Joining an ensemble with a chart full of notes and signs plonked in front of you. Hard Work!

The man who thought the whole world revolved around him

was in the middle of nowhere- it didn't really matter.

* * *

flashbacks

RED & ZMEN were recorded with my Red Music Man Silhouette, flame maple neck with two humbuckers and a single coil, loved that guitar it's feels, contour, flexibility. But the HK humid monsoonal weather used to fuck it up, through a Boss multi fx pedalboard no amps, as lugging around amps in HK was a "no no".

Once living back on Lamma Island I missed the ferry to Anders Nelson's Guangzhou gig-I had to get myself there, as I could, & I wasn't late for the soundcheck. Anders who knew Bruce was a bit pissed off.

IN GOD WE TRUST:

in music I didn't think too much, just do.

the clouds sprung across the sky, they didn't really seem to know where they were going. it didn't really matter.

Loved the atmosphere and feeling John Abercrombie evoked on his albums. Plus I loved his quartet. we got to hang in HK, Bruce Cale was the culprit, so I took John out all arvo on a scenic tour of HK, we also managed a jam /tutorial session back in his hotel room.

MY KUNG FU Music One ~ Australia

In the old days in Sydney, there was a vibe.

In my day as a novice performer – during the 1980's, I was again torn in a duality of pursuing Jazz vs. Pop. To be poor or earn some money was a factor too. In the Oz pop scene we had a number of local bands creating wonderful music, **The Church, Icehouse, Matt Finish** and specific songs immersed themselves in one's consciousness like Under the Milky Way, Short Note, Great South- ern Land, Cheap Wine and Evie. It may be ludicrous to say that **Midnight Oil, INXS** and **Cold Chisel** were the top three. I loved them, especially the first two. I'm talking 70's to 80's.

With the Sydney jazz scene we had the *Paradise Jazz Cellar* – where you could hear the likes of **Dale Barlow, The Benders, Mark Simmonds Freeboppers, James Morrison, Steve Brien, Robbie Krupski** and **Roger Frampton.** At the *Criterion Hotel* you had Joe "**BeBop**" **Lane** and his loyal entourage, or check out Crossfire at *The Basement* and **Kerrie Biddel** at *The Soup Plus.* It was a vibrant and exciting era along with other pioneering outfits around the scene like **Stepps, Jupiter, Pyramid, Sounds from Earth, Ayers Rock** and **The Free Beer Band, Nebula** all playing incredible music.

Growing up in the 60's was subjected to boredom and restraint as Australia was quite an isolated parochial place that no one ever much came to, especially famous creative artists. I somehow knew I'd never see Jimi Hendrix live, then he died same with Bruce Lee, so when I saw the film *Jimi Plays Berkeley* (where I would later go) on the big screen at a special Rock screening and pumped through a *mother fucka* sound system, I freaked. After seeing him in motion, I knew that's what I wanted to do. As much as I had heard that some guitar geniuses couldn't read music or had no training. I thought differently. This attitude helped me big time in sustaining a professional music career.

Jimi Hendrix: The most incredible musician ever. Fucken' oath. Totes blew me away. When Miles met Jimi...."*Yo Miles, you alien mofo, welcome to my club, we are both blues musicians, we took it into outer space*" "*Yo Miles, I don't know if I can get into this modal shit*" said the free spirited Sagittarius to the moody Gemini. There- fore nothing happened. Miles couldn't control it.

My next huge influence would be John McLaughlin, an Englishman and guitarist that exuded a gentlemanly aura of mysticism and clean living, plus technical prowess as a musician. Quite a different kettle of fish to Jimi who passed away at the age of 27. John still performs now in his 80's. When myself and fellow guitarist Peter Inglis were waiting in our concert seats for John to appear on stage at Sydney's State Theatre. *The One Truth Band* started up, but where is John? In this delirium, he suddenly appeared and we emitted loud sounds of complete hysteria "*ooo!!, aaahhh! eeee!!*" I had my walkman recorder and listening back it is hilarious. I now understood Beatle fans reactions at gigs. After the mind bending show we met John backstage. That changed my life. I met a hero!

Growing up in a fairly affluent suburb such as Mosman with hot guitarists like Dougle Brown and Macy in High School, I was totes taken by the **guitar** beginning with the Beatles, then finally succumbing to the flairs and magnetism of Jimi Hendrix.

By my mid teens, most of my high school friends in music and my- self (possibly due to hearing loss from measles medicine), gravitated more towards instrumental music. Hendrix's Electric LadyLand instrumental tracks "*Moon, Turn the Tides, Gently, Gently Away*", "*Rainy Day, Dream Away*" and Paul Kossof's "*Back Street Crawler*" along with Robin Trower became a staple diet, not to forget San- tana then Al Di Meola.

I loved Mosman and Mosman High School was a nurturing centre for music making. In music class initially we were all bored shitless with a classical repertoire. Later a new teacher with a beaut L series Stratocaster encouraged us. We dug him... Macy, Dougal Brown, Simon Baderle, Rolf Knudsen, Chris, me and Tony Buck, Doug Ironside, Brett Curotta, Ralph Hague all began performing and a healthy dose of competition and comradeship developed. Repertoire consisted mainly of Hendrix, Led Zeppelin, Santana. Along with originals. After my year in North America, I knew I want- ed to be a full time musician. By this age at 18 I was really a beginner. I left school, got a job at Berny's Radio and with some income was able to afford lessons with Peter Andrews at the Academy of Guitar in Bondi. Two years of this and I came out infatuated with fusion and with a keen desire to pursue jazz and chase gigs. I had developed my rock guitar style to a satisfactory level. Through my practise and study I found new chords on the guitar until I understood their structure. It was so exciting that I could create my own chords and voicings. During my day job at Bernys Radio, I met Midnight Oil guitarist Jim Moginie, saxophonist Paul Andrews & befriended Greg Sheehan. Paul really introduced me to Coltrane in his funky crib down at Mosman Bay near my house. Greg was this magnetic, inspiring hippy percussionist dude who was part of the band *Sounds from Earth*.

I co-formed a few groups with Chris Frazier, Tim Lumsdaine and Tony Buck for little gigs around the place. When I got out of Berklee College Boston and finally landed back in oz around 1981, I attended the Sydney Conservatorium Summer Jazz Clinic. We had a Hal Galper class, with which in addition to the stint at Berklee, I understood the importance of forward motion in phrasing and rhythmic placement. As I now hoped to fuse hard driving rock with jazz heavy metal bebop.

My study and the little time at Berklee, plus 9 hours practise a day, allowed me to tackle most musical situations. I immediately formed the "Guy Le Claire Quintet" with Steve Hunter (bass), Andrew Gander (drums), Jason Morphett (sax) and Kevin Hunt (piano/keys). An originals jazz group, we held a residency at "Jenny's Wine Bar" on Pitt St. I also recorded my stuff in the February of 1984.

https://guyleclaire.bandcamp.com/album/le-claire-quintet-rsvp-2

Now that I'm sixty, I can look back and see that my love affair with jazz didn't just begin with going to Berklee college of Music in Boston, it was sustained by the challenge it presented and all the wonderful, interesting, knowledgeable cats committed to the music. Grandpa Jack was an avid jazz fan, having over a thousand jazz recordings, he also took Mum to see Satchmo and a host of others thanks to the philanthropist Adelaide Boynthon family, Patrons of Jazz.

In a way I came upon jazz back to front. Immersed in Miles from *In A Silent Way* onto John Coltrane's *I Love Sydney.* That changed somewhat at Berklee with a chance meeting and jam in the Massachusetts Ave basement rooms with Kevin Daley, a very fine guitarist. These went well and he kept inviting me to jams. Finally my *one key* aptitudes ran out on standards like "*All The Things You Are*" as Kevin ripped and I flopped big time.

By passion, insight and exploring the traditions of *Trad, Bebop* to knowing *the standards repertoire*, I morphed.

Guitarists Mike Stern and John Scofield were huge influences. These two were already doing what I was thinking. I needed to learn it. Berklee gave me that impetus and direction.

Boxing day 26th December 2019...Listening to the Miles Davis box set I picked up in Lithgow. He finishes with his take on Cyndi Lauper's *Time after Time*, Fuck I miss that guy!. My plan was to get over to NY and join his band.

Band of Gypsy's "*Machine Gun*", the be all and end all of electric guitar.

"*Power of Soul*" Jimi is trying to encourage us "*with the power of soul, anything is possible*" or is that with the power of the Dole?

FB 1976

...Me and mum San Francisco. We're walking down the road in Berkeley CA and I see the place where Jimi Hendrix played "Hendrix in the West" album. His awesome rendition of Johnny. B Goode is going through my 16 year old mind. The footpath we're on, two gorgeous looking black chicks are approaching, Happy, they eye me off, smiling. My little willy is blushing...

By the mid 1980's, I was touring all over Australia in very well known bands *Eurogliders, Ian Moss Band, Matt Finish* and free- lancing as a session muso plus teaching privately also. However, by the end of that decade I was burnt out. In search of respite, the family relocated to the Blue Mountains (100 km's west of Sydney). All of us including my stroker Dad lived there which was good, however the arse had fallen out of the live music scene, and I worried about the mortgage. In 1991, I released my self titled debut GUY LE CLAIRE on CD independently and received some very good press from the media. As a result I was offered "Head of the guitar Department" at AIM (Australian Institute of Music) in Sydney. I then commuted 5 days week on the 2 hour train trip from Katoomba to Central. In all this I put some bands together. Faves being *Them Or Us* with Geoff Lungren and Bill Heckenberg, GleC and the *Frank Sonatas* with Chris Frazier, Warren Trout and Bill Risby, *Playdiem* with Steve Hunter, David Jones and John Foreman. Zilch mountain band with Boof, Gary Evans and Frank Corby. Having bassist, jazz master and Blue Mountains resident Bruce Cale as a mentor enabled me to study and play with a real jazzer. In fact we got on so well as people and players, we ended up holding a weekend residency gig (Fri/Sat) as a jazz duo at the Hillcrest Coachman in Leura for two years, culminating in a Wangaratta Jazz appearance and a CD. With Bruce, the beauty for me was to get *outside of my head and play! Just play it!* That way it begins to internalise. This experience would set me up well for future gigs in HK.

I've had the good fortune of playing with many great Australian Musoz, such as Dale Barlow, Jonathan Zwartz, Matt McMahon, Hamish Stuart, Tim Bruer, Alex Hewetson, Paul Joseph, Paul Andrews (RIP), Sandy Evans, Peter Dehlsen, Jeremy Sawkins, Azo Bell, Tim Rollinson, John Prior, LIndsay Jehan, Kevin Borich, Dave Adams, Harry Brus, Rebecca Johnson, Rex Goh, Phil Witcher, Peter Northcote, Sam McNally, Steve Sowerby, John 'Watto' Watson, Mark Kennedy, Armando Hurley, Mark Costa, Alan Dargin, Chong Lim, Don Reid, Mark Riley, Jan Preston, Gary Evans, Mina, Paul Najar, Justin Dileo, Maddy and Mick Young, Ian Belton, Steve Fearnley, Dave Colton, Stan Mobbs, Steve Prestwich, Will Scarlett, Mike Hague, Grace Knight, Bernie Lynch, Chris Sweeny, Steve Merta, Bob Wynyard, Dario Bortolin, Gordon Rytmeister and Dave Addis. The list is extensive though I may have missed some talent.

MY KUNG FU Music ~ Hong Kong

As I've mentioned earlier, hopping up on stage in Hong Kong to sit in with a band was not frowned upon, in many ways it was welcomed. It broke the monotony of Hong Kong gigdom and the musicians were interested to hear what you did. So armed with new business cards, I jumped up wherever possible and that my friends led to many gig offers. I got very busy pretty quickly.

All my Aussie pro gig experience helped me in business and dealings with musicians. I formed the first of many bands here, the Guy Le Claire Trio with Peter Scherr on double bass and Anthony Fernandes on drums. We recorded our gig at the HK Jazz Club and I released it independently. That CD was well received and placed me into some media spotlight and inherent local musical gossip. More and more gigs came, sometimes three a day, this lasted over 2 decades playing with luminaries Allen Youngblood, Justin Siu, Blaine Whittaker, Mark Henderson, Flynn Adams, Eugene Pao, Larry Hammond, Peter Scherr, Elaine Liu, Johnny Fuego, Gemma & Jondi Mac, Ted Lo, Bob Mocarsky, Rickard Malmsten, Paul Candelaria, Jnr Carpio and Johnny, Skip Moy, Sylvain Gagnon, Howard McCrary, Michael Wong, Oliver Smith(le French trio not from France/*muaarggghhh*) and fulfilling Jazz Club residencies performing with imported American Blues acts such as Phil Guy, Guitar Shorty, Eddie King and Luther Guitar Junior Johnson to name some...

By the early 2000's I was touring world-wide with HK pop stars (Canto/Mando pop). These were high level reading gigs, luckily my reading had blossomed but the tricky rhythmic phrases on paper were doing my head in. I diverted to Konokol, the traditional Indian music science and found that the tricky semi quavers were singable therefore playable. These gigs paid well. There was no time for kung fu training.

As was my routine, I completed my usual cycle of *work hard - burn out - retire to get energy back*. In an attempt to break this cycle, I settled in the outer Hong Kong area, Clearwater Bay. I was looking to build my private teaching business up. Along with very enjoyable teaching sessions with top students Ron Ng, Daniel Ng (no direct relations) along with Dr John Chung, Gary Seib, Jerry Smith and Luke Riggs(Luke inherited my Ibanez RG550), Nathan Lam, Jack Bojan, brothers Saxon and Jarvis Whittaker, Olivia and Liam Paige. I began enjoying the teaching process and the little business prospered.

I must say it was a joy to be playing alongside great HK musoz as mentioned previously - adding to that list: Jason Ho, Skip Moy, Rudy Balbuena, Dodong Fuego, Joey Villanueva, Paul Candelaria, Justin Siu, Choi A Kun, Anthony Leung, Roel Garcia, DC, Paul Levi, Mark Peter, Tom Tse, Siraj, John Von Seggern, Jun Kung, Angelita Li, Jezreal Lucero, Sidwell O Neil, Joe Rosenberg, Steve Sacks, ABA, Kai Djuric, Ginger Kwan, Donald Ashley, Tommy Ho, Benjamin Li, Joyce Peng, Gaz Selb, Jez Smith, Mike Carr, Balu, Gary Da Silva, Brigitte Mitchell, Oz Walker, Franklin Torres, Tom Nunan, Jim Schneider, Michelle Carillo, Dan LaVelle, LeLe, Zhang Zhi Yong, Ted Lo, Rob Scott, The Carpios, Yip Dak Han, Anthony Lun, Tsai Qin, Sally and George Lam, Faye Wong, Peter Lee, Joao Mascaranhas, Chinda, Miles Li, Kenny Matsura, Jason Cheng, Mano Manolette, Wink Vastine Pettis, Charlie Huntley, Chris Polanco, Joel Haggard, Dave Packer, Dale Wilson, Cary Abrahams, Jamie Murcell, Melchoir, The Aranas Quincy/Ricky, Chris Collins, Les Fong, Jeff Young, Bob Mocarsky, Ray Covington, Nicholas McBride, Nicholas Bouloukos, Gilbert Caselis, Michael Wong, David Tong, Charlie Foldesh, Howard McCrary, Mike Carr, Stephen Ives, Tim Wilson, Winnie Chung, Sybil Thomas, Manuela Lo, Pierre Veniot, Pete Kelly, Neil Irwin plus all the musoz who played in my bands or I played with in their bands...Rickard maintained a Tuesday night I was part of for a good long while, Bob Mocarskey put together his organ trio Thurs at Joyce is not here I also was part of, Justin Siu put together an interesting China/Western ensemble in Pacific Place, with my own gigs, often i was juggling three gigs a day - this gave me a good income, but Boy you worked bloody hard! Tuesday night residency at the Bohemian lounge (Rickard Malmsten/Mark Peter and Rick's Elements shopping centre day gigs, I had regular Weds with Linus Why & brother Robbin at Geckos. In addition I frequently joined Eugene Pao's Rock tribute at the Jazz Club-Sats. with the great Jun Kung-drums and Angelita Li-vocals. we used to rip that up!. and with Blaine and Allen Youngblood at the Foreign Corespondents Club 2-3 times a week. What a fucking scene!

Not to forget Sunday arvoz with Z-MEN (Flynn, Robbin, Guy) at Mes Amis. Plus I was the MD for Swire group's Pacific Place Swire plaza providing music Fri & Sat. strategically booking acts that I may be able to play in to expand my music horizons. it MD for trendy restaurant 'Blue' in SoHo HK, playing lunches.

.In fact..Aussie musicians are recruited by me in Hong Kong, (or if they are passing through), I set up gigs for Dale Barlow, Steve Hunter, Scott Tinkler, brother Chris Frazier, Walter Lampe, Tony Buck, Peter Knight, and Andy Gander...

Everything ended with falling sick, and the forced return back home.

In my musical career, I had the energy to form a number of bands, not in chronology, only as I remember

Guy Le Claire Quintet ~

Steve Hunter, Jason Morphett, Andy Gander, Kevin Hunt.

Guy Le Claire and the Frank Sonatas ~

Chris Frazier, Warren Trout, Bill Risby.

Guy Le Claire Trio ~ Peter Scherr, Anthony Fernandes.

Guy Le Claire Trio 2 ~ Scott Dodd, Robbin Harris.

Z-MEN ~ Robbin Harris and Flynn Adams.

Bruce Cale with Guy Le Claire ~ Duo

Zilch ~ Gary Evans, Frank Corby, Boof – Ray Husband

Guy Le Claire ~ John Prior, Lindsay Jehan.

Alchemy ~ Linus Why, Robbin Harris, Jondi Mac, Mark Hender- son.

World Project ~ Tom Tse, Siraj, Cameron Reid, Sylvain Gagnon, Zhang Zhi Yong.

Playdiem ~ David Jones, Steve Hunter, John Foreman.

RED ~ Peter Scherr, Andrew Collier.

Compadres ~ Esteban Antonio and Guy Le Claire duo.

FUNFF ~ Blaine Whittaker, Robbin Harris, Sebastien Meyer.

Them Or Us ~ Geoff Lungren, Bill Heckenberg.

Selected CD Covers

Selected CD Covers

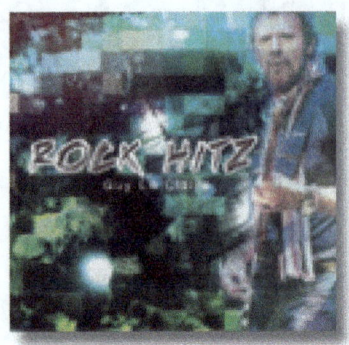

Selected Discography:

* Guy Le Claire Quintet: RSVP 1984 (Cassette only Release)

* Playdiem - Playdiem (Larriikin LRJ 329) 1994 CD

* Guy Le Claire (GLC 001) 1991 CD (Out of Print)

* Guy Le Claire Trio Live (3-logic-music 003) 1997 CD (Out of Print) * Guy Le Claire - Plonk with Scott Tinkler, Larry Hammond, Allen Youngblood (GLC 005) 1999 CD (Out of Print)

* Guy Le Claire & Bruce Cale –Standard Time 2002 CD(Out of Print) * Guy Le Claire - Xin Xin Solo 2002 CD (Out of Print)

* Guy Le Claire - Red (3-logic-music 007) 2003 CD (Out of Print)

* Z-Men - Z-MEN 2003 CD (Out of Print)

* Guy Le Claire ROCK HITZ (3-logic-music 010) 2013 * Guy Le Claire Trio 2 (3-logic-music 009) 2013 CD

* Guy Le Claire Solo 3 (3-logic-music 011) 2013 CD

2 CDs are currently available to buy and download:

from Amazon or eBay.

Guy Le Claire ~ *Solo 3* Guy Le Claire ~ *Trio 2*

Or go to the web address below for mp3's of most of the above selections and more.

https://guyleclaire.bandcamp.com/

I couldn't say there is/was a thread or commonality between HK and Aus musically speaking. HKers tend to like soothing harmonious music/Yin, where as Aussies like muscle and power/Yang. Each flourished on it's own.

GO BACK YOU ARE GOING THE WRONG WAY

Back in Australia 2016 to the end.

I say "experience as much as possible(within reason) and put it in your music. You can do it! Music is really a simple thing - a reflection of life."

the robots are taking over, enjoy life while you can.

Leigh's in hospital, a Moe boy bra bra he said "the blues comes from your boots" the Black Duck lives.

Leigh died yesterday 22/07/21, due to health issues, complications, inoperable from acute alcoholism. RIP Mate.The ole jb & coke finally got him… however the black duck from Moe Vic, did have his morals and values.. buying Australian all the way, slumberland, Telstra, AGL, he aspired to a comfortable life and passed on comfortably in hospital.

MY KUNG FU Mos Def

Baba-baba-baba-baba-baba, you been so good to me

When I was a little boy you were the only one I wanted to be

To be like pa duke and ma duke

How much I love the both of you

I know all the strain we been through

But it's of no consequence cause we're comin through

[VERSE 1: Mos Def]

Check it

I first studied my kung fu in the Brakalak

In the center of (?) inside that old street shack

This had to be about ten years back

Before I ever even heard of a 24 track

Talkin about you as an MC was not the move

Cause if you said you had skill, well then you had to show and prove

And if there ever was a party, son yo, I would set it

And tell the DJ run the beat from (Ultra-magnetic)

I grab the mic and then I leave the party buzzin

Tellin all the honeys I was Slick Rick's cousin

When they knew I wasn't, but I had no shame

Pa, you know the name, the Mos always had game

Back in the day of the Rap Attack

When brothers knew how to act, before Glocks and crack

And Vandy C was doin radio shows

And 'crossover' meant that you wore your mom's clothes

When Sweet G was talkin about the games that people play

I used to sit back and say: yeah indeed, someday

And as I grew older my kung fu grew better

Instead of shootin the humbles I was shootin all nets

And now my time has come

And now hip-hop's an industry polluted by bums

Posin with guns, they're puffin mad blunts

Aiyo, brothers just started rhymin last month

They gettin fat deals on any major label

When they only seen other people hold the mic cable

Five years ago when we was dancin house

When the DJ played hip-hop, then you walked out

But now you're hard, talkin about you paid mad dues

I used to see your ass abused wearin platform shoes

I ain't confused, who you think you're foolin with that get-up?

You ain't genuine, so don't waste your time

Riffin over here cause there ain't no chance

That you could break the sound, son, you ain't that advanced

Times are gettin critical across the land

Don't provide the b-boy, introduce the b-man - understand?

The M-o-s D is who I am, now check it out, y'all

[Hook]

My kung fu is the style you haven't mastered

[VERSE 2: DCQ]

At the age of 18 made a little money

And I needed some advice on how to live my life

Was goin through strife, people couldn't understand

That I was comin into my own, becomin a man

I had to have a plan cause I know what I'm here for

So I can't waste time, y'all

Gotta be on the ball and represent for my peeps

(Where?) In the streets!

I make beats and kick facts over fat tracks

It's all of that from the Brakalak

Goin through problems as a adolescent

A lot of troubles and turmoils, there was persistence

And I know that I stutter

But it don't matter cause I'm a bad -

I flip a verse either backwards, sideways

I rocks my [edited] from here, Mondays, Fridays

Saturdays and I get a weekend off

My [edited] ain't soft

(Well, excuse me, baby)

You paid your dues cause I'm the boss

So mother[edited] Bruce Springsteen and Diana Ross

Because they know what the time is

I rock [edited] for the fly kids, b-men, bouncin bass bombastics

Kick it drastic, you get tossed like an ash, kid

Youknowmsayin?

[Hook]

[VERSE 3: Ces]

Well, I'm sleek and I freak a beat

For you and your peeps to bump inside your jeeps

Your Acura, Honda or whatever

Bump it in the Benzi and get your head together

Strollin down the F.D.R

Playin the microphone star

Deep in your car

With the thump-diddy-thump-da-thump-da-thump-thump

Pop up the trunk and let the bass bump

If you ain't got a ride, well, that's alright

Let the U keep you company on your hike

Trekin down the ave with your headphones on

Take em off for a sec, you still feel gone

You're pressin rewind, many, many times

I must rock the mic cause it's only right

Comin right up off of Eastern ground

This is how you get down, I hope you like the sound

Thermo offering number one

There's more in store, there's more to come

We far from done, no, the show ain't over

So when we comin through, don't say I never told ya.

parking on the left

* * *

Some of my Best Gigs:

1.**With Josh** in YS China American Josh came up with 'fake as fuck' - FAF/ i came up with 'real as fuck' - RAF, he restructured Dylan's Mississippi, to 'stayed in Yangshuo way too long'.

2. **Funff**- my band of Blaine Whitaker-alto, Robbin Harris-drums and

Sebastien Meyer-upright. Awesome venue in Zhuhai China put together by Peter Lee, we were treated like "rock stars" and the music was good too.

3. **solo JZ bar Shanghai**-my solo performance in a foreign city, where I met drummer Al Gordon.

4.**Deanie Yip Dak Han** (Cantonese Celebrity)-proved music is an international language. An emotional engrossing concert covering the popular musical spectrum with the brilliant Anthony Lun- MD/piano, Anthony Fernandes-drums, Rudy Balbuena-bass, Joey Villanueva-guitar, Wink Vastine Petits and Charlie Huntley-horns et moi.

5.Brickhouse-Commodores bassist Ronald La Preu funks up Hong Kong avec moi, Robbin Harris-drums and genius Jezreal Lucero-keys. Best funkin' ever!

6. **Playdiem** gigs at the Harbourside Brasserie and Basement, with Steve Hunter and David Jones roaring like a lion behind me. scare wee

7. Blaine Whittaker's **Austet**, this was a fun gig celebrating a union of Aussie jazzers at Peel Fresco Soho, Hong Kong. Blaine ,moi, Scott Dodd, Nicholas McBride.

8. **Zilch** at Hotel Alex with Boof stage diving / mosh pit into the crowd of his mates at front of stage, they all split and Boof landed 'thunk thunk thunk' on the dance floor. hilarious at the time, while I was squirming around my rig feedbacking while Gary and Frank powered as a rhythm section!

9. Macau - **History of Rock**-school show put together by Samantha Fitchett Vogee, showcasing the story of western popular music featuring talented and attractive British actors /actresses/ singers. In Macau on this occasion the kids went crazy storming the stage, moi, Robbin, Jezreal and Franklin Torres-bass didn't quite know what to do.

11. Aunty Eds **Bruce Cale and GleC**. After having not played together for a few years, and me living in Hong Kong playing lots of jazz. Bruce and I hit the stage in Katoomba with Colin Day in attendance doing the sound we played beautifully.

12. **Esteban gig 'Compadres'**. just me and Esteban Antonio on acoustic

KIF guitars. Magical gig with visuals and substance in the Fringe Theatre Hong Kong.

13. **Mark Henderson's Soul 5.**- Mark put the funkiest unit together avec moi, Rob Scott-bass. and some other negroes we were to open a new club in Beijing, we played the opening night, afterwhich the Beijinger and Shanghainese bosses fell out big time. We were told to chill for the next week all expenses paid. So with our soul/funk vibe we hit on the cool little music venues in Beijing, eventually jamming with Cui Jian (China's Rock godfather).

14. **Robert Lucas** - Canned Heat singer came over for a 7 day engagement at the Hong Kong Jazz Club, Simon Barker - drums and I did it. A week of Blues and Fun!

top performances attended:

1. Temple drummers of Kerala-HK Cultural Centre

2. Joe Henderson- HK cultural centre

3. Joshua Redman- HKcultural centre

4. One Truth Band-State Theatre, Sydney

5. Midnight Oil-Royal Antler, Narrrabeen

6. George Benson-State Theatre

GUITARISTS in the last decade and a half

1. Kurt Rosenwinkel – nuts about this guy can't get his music out of this old head.

35. Jonathan Kriesberg – beautiful player.

36. Peter Bernstein

37. Wayne Krantz

38. James Muller

39. James Sherlock

40. Steve Magnussen

41. Eugene Pao
42. Tossin Abasi
43. Gary Clark Jnr
44. John Frusciante
45. Derek Trucks
46. Ulf Wakenius

ARE WE THERE YET?

RE-GEAR.

FOR GUITARISTS THE PALETTE AVAILABLE TO ALTER SOUNDS IS INCREDIBLE, MY WHOLE ALIEN SPACESHIP SERIES IS BASED ON THE Me-80 FX I WAS ABLE TO CONJURE UP. FX HAVE BECOME AN INSTRUMENT, REALLY. IT TAKES ARTISTIC JUDGEMENT TO

PROCREATE/ARRANGE SOUNDS ETC. ALL MUSICAL INSTRUMENTS CAN NOW BE AFFECTED BY THIS 2ND INSTRUMENT. I LOOK FORWARD TO WORKING WITH MY VOICE ALONG WITH GUITAR AND FX. THANK YOU

I ACKNOWLEDGE THE TRIBES AND TRIBAL ELDERS OF THIS LAND.

https://guyleclaire.bandcamp.com/album/guy-le-claire-solo-2-in-an-alien-spaceship

I LOVE MY WIFE ISTRIKU, BELLISA EVANS GUNADHI LE CLAIRE XXX`

* * *

RETIRED PROFESSIONAL AUSTRALIAN / HONG KONG GUITAR MAN AND CHINESE KUNG FU ENTHUSIAST,

GUY LE CLAIRE SHARES HIS THOUGHTS AND EXPERIENCES, ALONG WITH HISTORY IN THIS RIVETING READ. Guy wrote his first book "My Kung Fu- Stroke" in Hong Kong, finally collaborating with Chris Frazier and finishing the book in Australia. his entire Music Catalogue sits at guyleclaire.bandcamp.com

Guy talks about a professional musicians life from the 60s to 2000s spanning Australia, Hong Kong & China his bases. Filled with experience, his story shines.

I'd like to thank Leigh Johnston, Olaf and Samantha Vogee, Bellisa Evans, My Mum - Carolle Boyce, Dad - Guy senior,

Ma Li Yin, Kez, Simone Barry, NDIS, Peter Watson, Dr. Philip Penfold, Steve Merta, Paul Chow, Rickard Malmsten, John Prior, Lindsay Jehan, brothers Chris Frazier, Robbin Harris, Flynn Adams and all the Musicians!

The people of Australia and Hong Kong - ga la wor!

Guy Le Claire has a certificate of Music from Berklee College of Music. Boston.

A Diploma of music from the Australian Institute of Music. Sydney.

A Jazz Guitar Performance Diploma from The London College of Music.

He deffered his Masters of Music UNSW study to pursue lucrative performance career all over Asia where he also created a teaching base succesfully. Guy's teaching began 50 years ago in Sydney's North Shore, escalating to Head of Guitar at the Australian Institute of Music his experience is invaluable with high encouragement to students. His near 30 years in Hong Kong, he suffered a couple of strokes in 2014 retreating back to Australia in 2015, he teaches a little guitar & taichi qi gong.

But, At the day with the going down of the sun, we shall remember them.guyleclairemusic@outlook.com

ARE WE THERE YET? WHERE ARE WE?

OUR BEAUTIFUL PLANET IS DYING, PLEASE BE AWARE OF MOTHER EARTH, WIPE NEGLIGENCE & IGNORANCE AWAY. RECYCLE, PLANT, REJUVENATE, THINK " AM I CORRECT IN THIS ACTION HERE?' GOOD LUCK!!!

THE END

I have realised what is to be realised, I have developed what is to be developed, I have eliminated what is to be eliminated, therefore Brahmana I am the Buddha.

Quote of Shakyamuni Buddha. wasn't me!

Retired professional musician/guitarist writes his musical memoir of 40 years, primarily centred in Australian & Hong Kong after a Stroke forces him to withdraw from performance. Ranging from the 1960's to 2015, Guy talks music, gear, styles, history & acting roles.

Guy Le Claire19/09/23